'EUROCOMMUNISM'

IMPLICATIONS FOR EAST AND WEST

'EUROCOMMUNISM'

Implications for East and West

by

Roy Godson
Stephen Haseler

Research Contributors

Leonard Schapiro — Annie Kriegel — Giuseppe Are
François Bourricaud — Rui Machete — Eusebio Mujal-Leon

First published 1978 by
THE MACMILLAN PRESS LTD
London and Basingstoke
Associated companies in Delhi
Dublin Hong Kong Johannesburg Lagos
Melbourne New York Singapore Tokyo

Typeset in Great Britain by
Santype International Ltd, Salisbury
and printed in Great Britain

British Library Cataloguing in Publication Data

Godson, Roy
'Eurocommunism'
1. Communist parties
2. Political parties—Europe
I. Title   II. Haseler, Stephen
329'.02'094   JN94.A979

ISBN 0-333-25675-1
ISBN 0-333-25677-8   Pbk

PSOE   (Spanish) Socialist (Workers) Party
PSP   Socialist Party (Spain)
SPD   Social Democratic Party (Federal Republic of Germany)
TASS   News Service of the Soviet Union
TUC   Trades Union Congress (Great Britain)
USSR   Union of Soviet Socialist Republics
WFTU   World Federation of Trade Unions

To
Frank, Ed and Frank
and others who care

Contents

vii

List of Abbreviations

AFL–CIO American Federation of Labor and Congress of Industrial Organizations
DC Christian Democratic Party (Italy)
CGIL Italian General Confederation of Labour
CGT General Confederation of Workers (France)
CGTP–IN Intersindical—General Confederation of Workers (Portugal)
COMECON Council for Mutual Economic Assistance
CP Communist Party
CPGB Communist Party of Great Britain
CPSU Communist Party of the Soviet Union
DKP German Communist Party (Federal Republic of Germany)
EC European Communities (European Atomic Energy Community, European Coal and Steel Community, and European Economic Community)
EEC European Economic Community
FDP Free Democratic Party (Federal Republic of Germany)
FNLA National Front for the Liberation of Angola
GDR German Democratic Republic
KGB Committee of State Security of the Soviet Union
MFA Armed Forces Movement (Portugal)
MP Member of Parliament
MSI Italian Social Movement (neo-Fascist)
NATO North Atlantic Treaty Organization
PCE (Spanish) Communist Party
PCF (French) Communist Party
PCI (Italian) Communist Party
PCP (Portuguese) Communist Party
PLO Palestine Liberation Organization

Introduction

Thirty years after their expulsion from government, and their consignment to the fringes of European politics, the major Communist parties of Western Europe are serious contenders for political power. They are also the subjects of a widespread reassessment. Scholars and politicians, on both sides of the Atlantic, hold contrasting views about this controversial political phenomenon. Broadly, there are two polar perspectives.

First, there are those who hold that little has changed since the days of the Comintern and Cominform; that the major West European Communist parties remain totalitarian and subservient to Soviet interests, little more than an arm of Soviet international power. From this perspective the growth of Communist parties in Western Europe is seen as an unmixed blessing for the Kremlin. Secondly, an alternative view is that the West European Communist parties have either so radically changed, or are now so constrained that they pose little or no threat to the democracies of Western Europe or to the stability of the Western alliance. Indeed, as alternative 'liberal' models, they represent a distinct danger to the Soviet Politburo's control of Eastern Europe and the Soviet Union.

This study maintains that the first thesis is overdrawn, but that the second is speculative and mistaken. Certainly, there have been significant changes in the Communist parties over the last two decades, and further evolution cannot be ruled out. Moreover, the relationship between the Kremlin and the Communist parties is more complex than in the 1930s and 1940s, and, in some important respects, unwelcome in Moscow. Even so, developments both within the parties, and between them and Moscow, until now have not proceeded to the point where a break with the past can sensibly be attested to. The Communist parties, as they themselves point out, are still committed to many of the fundamental postulates of Marxism–Leninism; they remain decidedly 'illiberal' in their internal party organization; and even their recently revised economic and social policy objectives would pose a serious threat to pluralism and representative democracy. Also, the parties, notwithstanding differences of opinion with Moscow, remain decidedly pro-Soviet in foreign policy matters— particularly outside Europe. Consequently, the increasing strength of these parties shifts the balance of power in the direction of the Soviet Union, without correspondingly weakening the Kremlin's control over Eastern Europe and the Soviet Union.

Therefore, to view the Communists' entry as major partners into Western European governments with equanimity (or even with mild, tempered concern) is too complacent. Such a development would represent a sea–change of historic proportions, unsettling to the post-war political consensus of the Western European continent. It would be destabilizing in that it would tend to detach Western Europe from the United States, leaving the Soviet Union as the only major power on the European continent. The resultant power vacuum would be a threat to the peace in one of the most important democratic and industrially powerful regions of the world.

The West's response to West European Communism, however, should be subtle. Only the peoples of the various West European nations can determine the future of their own societies. Even so, there is abundant evidence that even in the countries most vulnerable to Communist advance, public opinion, even amongst those who sometimes vote Communist, remains firmly hostile to Marxism–Leninism. Neither the United States nor the West European democratic parties should necessarily shut the door to dialogue and debate with the Communist parties. On the contrary, a heightened ideological and philosophical contest may be in the West's interest.

For example, by insisting that the European Communist

parties demonstrate their loyalty to democracy and human rights, they may be led to condemn Soviet control of Eastern Europe, support liberal elements in those countries, and even attempt a further 'liberalization' of their governing ideology. We believe this to be an unlikely development, but one that should be encouraged. If the Communist parties do move in a more 'liberal' direction, and break with the Soviets, then this would serve to weaken them by splitting the militants loyal to the Soviet Union and ideological orthodoxy from the more 'reformist' elements which might in turn encourage the 'reformists' to develop into democratic socialists. It would also encourage further strains in the relations between the Communist parties and the Soviet Union, as well as encourage liberal and dissident forces under Soviet control.

Whilst continuing to isolate the Communists from power, the West should encourage change within the Communist parties so that it can exploit the tension between the Communist parties and Moscow. The specific tactics that should be employed to achieve this objective await further study. This study does not include a list of detailed policy suggestions—apart, that is, from a plea for a renewed Western political initiative which can build upon a coherent Western policy of 'Human Rights.'

This study focuses, for the most part, on the Southern European Communist parties. These parties are large and well organized. They have significant electoral support which may well continue to grow. Some of them may be about to participate in government. In addition, they control sizeable sectors of the labour movement, and other strategic non-governmental sectors (including the media), which accrue to them considerable extra-parliamentary leverage over their societies. Also, the leadership of three of these parties (the Italian, French and Spanish) has been in the vanguard of change, both domestically and in their relationship towards the Soviet Union. These developments have given rise to the commonly used term: 'Eurocommunism.' If a new Communist phenomenon is indeed emerging in Western Europe, then it should manifest itself most markedly in these parties. If not, then it is unlikely that it will be present elsewhere in Western Europe, in the smaller and weaker parties. Thus, a study of the Southern European parties has a more general application to the rest of the western continent.

In addition to the Southern European parties, this study also explores developments within the Communist party of one 'northern' nation, Great Britain. As British Foreign Minister David Owen has suggested, the British Communist Party remains influential.[1] Although miniscule electorally, it has a significant influence within the powerful British trade union movement. Although the precise extent of this influence is difficult to determine, the British Communist Party remains a political and industrial force that any British government, Labour or Conservative, must be concerned with. Also the British Communist Party has recently made overtures for greater collaboration with the Labour Party—a collaboration which the dominant left wing within the Labour Party apparatus does not appear to resist as strenuously as did its social democratic predecessors. The British Communist Party, in line with some of the Southern European parties, has changed somewhat of late—both domestically and in its relations with the Soviet Union, a process resulting in the departure of some of its Stalinist militants. Developments within the British party are not only of interest to students of European politics and Atlantic co-operation; they also illustrate some of the dilemmas facing other small 'minor' Communist parties in Northern Europe.

The term 'Eurocommunism' is used sparingly in this text. This term tends to assume that the West European Communist parties have already developed a type of Communism that is radically divergent from that in force throughout the Soviet Union and Eastern Europe. Also, it implies the arrival of a new political phenomenon arising out of the Western tradition. Yet, while there have indeed been variations in doctrine and in attitudes towards Soviet hegemony of the international Communist movement, such subtle departures from orthodoxy cannot as yet, in our view, lead to their being dignified as a wholly new political category, indigenous to Western Europe, unlinked to the Communist past and experience in the Soviet sphere.

Secondly, 'Eurocommunism' implies a pan-Western European movement, a uniformity of ideological and political development amongst the various Communist parties. Yet, as is discussed in the text, there are continuing substantial differences between the various Communist parties, not only between North and South (the 'mass' and 'minor') parties, but between the Latin parties themselves. Certainly, the Spanish Communist Party, particularly in the personage of its leader, Santiago Carrillo, exhibits a political fluidity that may develop into a 'new' kind of Communism; yet Carrillo's apparent 'liberality' is not particularly infectious, certainly not so in the rest of Iberia, nor in France, and not even in Italy. Hence, the use of a term that suggests that a new Communist phenomenon is spread widely and evenly throughout the variegated Communist parties of Western Europe obscures more than it reveals.

Rather than rely upon a number of standard but dated secondary works by American and European academics, the authors, under the auspices of the Georgetown University International Labor Program and the National Strategy Information Center,[2] commissioned a series of background papers from prominent European scholars. The European scholars, from different countries, generations and of differing political persuasions, were asked to respond to a list of questions about trends in the various European Communist parties and their implications for domestic politics and for East and West (see the appendix for brief résumés of the European scholars). These background papers were written in the late autumn of 1977 and the data incorporated into the present study in the spring of 1978. The authors of this book are indebted to the European contributors. The authors are also indebted to Frank Barnett, Frank Trager, Dorothy Nicolosi, William Douglas, Sven Kraemer, and Bob Schuettinger, as well as Charlotte Kraatz, for their invaluable assistance. However, the authors alone assume responsibility for the facts, arguments and conclusions in the study.

The book is divided into three parts. Chapter One, essentially a factual survey, looks at the strength of Communism in Western Europe. It attempts an assessment of the size, power and influence of the major selected Communist parties through an analysis of trends in the Communist parties' membership, electoral and industrial base. It also attempts to give some tentative reasons for the recent growth of the Communist phenomenon in Western Europe.

Chapter Two is concerned with the Communist parties

and domestic politics. Here, the overriding concern is the
extent to which the CPs are a threat to the democratic
order. This part begins with a discussion of the ultimate
aims of the Communist Parties, their strategy and internal
workings (the practice of 'democratic centralism'), and proceeds to an analysis of the Communist Party's 'alliance' policy
with other parties and forces. It then analyses the whole
conglomeration of claims made by the Communists about
the protection of freedoms and democratic pluralism, about
public ownership and the relations of trade unions to the
state under Communist rule. Declaratory positions are described, Party by Party, and compared with Communist practice and theory. In this part of the book, an attempt is
made to determine whether, should the Communists come
to power, Communist governments would represent a clear
break with the post-war democratic and pro-Western political
consensus of Western Europe.

Chapter Three deals with the implications of the growth
of West European Communism for the international balance
between East and West. It looks, in turn, at co-operation
and conflict between the Soviet Union and the Communist
Parties, and the implications of Communist perspectives on
European unity and NATO. It comes to a conclusion about
the effect that Communist or Communist-influenced governments would have upon the international balance and suggests
some tentative recommendations about the West's response
to the growth of Communism in Europe.

1 The Strength of Communist Parties in Western Europe

AN OVERVIEW

Whichever way one wishes to measure Communist power and influence in Western Europe (by votes, party membership figures or party control of non-governmental institutions) one cannot avoid the conclusion that Communism is still a minority phenomenon. Taken overall, West Europeans remain a non-Communist—even an anti-Communist—people.

In terms of votes cast at elections, still the best guide of popular opinion, West European Communism attracts far less support than either the parties of the centre-right (Christian Democrats, Gaullists, Conservatives) or the parties of the centre-left (British Labour, West German SPD, Spanish and Portuguese Socialists and related parties of the Socialist International). Essentially, the West European Communist parties vie with the relatively small parties of Liberalism[1] for the position of the third largest electoral force on the western continent, with 10–12% of the total West European vote.

Communist parties can expect, at the very best, no more than 15% of the seats in the projected direct elections to the European Parliament. It has been estimated[2] that the Communist parties will gain no more than 49 out of the 410 seats in these forthcoming elections. If Spain and Portugal were to be admitted to the Community, then the CPs would gain an (estimated) 57 seats out of an (estimated) 483-seat chamber.[3]

Even in the four Southern European nations, where the Communist vote is concentrated (France, Italy, Portugal and Spain), the Communists only managed, at the most recent parliamentary elections, to gain an average of about 20% of the total votes cast.[4] Even in Italy and France, the electoral success of the Communist parties should be set in perspective. At the last elections in Italy, 65.6% of the voting public rejected the PCI. In France, those rejecting the PCF in 1978 amounted, on the first ballot, to 79.4% of the electorate.

Communist party membership figures in Italy and France are impressive, particularly in the light of the disciplined nature of the party organizations. However, the increasingly high 'turn-over rate' of the membership, particularly that of the PCF, must raise some questions about their future cohesion. Also, there is no evidence that the Latin Communist parties are a particularly attractive political magnet for the younger generations, even less so for women.

The Communists have a considerable influence in a number of important non-governmental social, economic and cultural sectors and are seeking to expand their influence in key institutions in their respective states. It is within the trade union movements that the Communists appear to have made most headway, but there are still powerful centres of trade union resistance to the various CPs in all the West European nations. Except for Portugal, there is no West European nation of which it can fairly be claimed that the Communist party has complete control over most strategic centres of trade union power. Furthermore, most trade unionists in Western Europe as a whole are not Communists and do not even sympathize with Communist parties. Even in France and Italy, a union member in a Communist-controlled union does not necessarily identify with the Communist party.

It is when one looks at the dynamics of West European political development that the growth of the Communist phenomenon becomes more apparent. In Italy and France, arguably in Portugal, and potentially in Spain, Communist parties are major political actors with every chance of moving to the centre of the stage, either as leading men or in highly featured supporting roles. In Italy, the PCI, although attracting just over a third of the vote, has almost doubled the percentage of votes it received in the late 1940s—to the point where it is now generally believed that stable government in Italy can only be carried on with its assent. Indeed, as Altiero Spinelli, one of the Italian founding fathers of the Common Market, has said: 'The Italian Communist Party . . . is an organic element of our political thinking and political culture . . . it is physiologically a large part of Italian reality.'[5] This kind of resigned realism was not current in the forties, fifties or sixties.

In France, although the PCF seems stuck upon a electoral plateau of about 20% of the vote (a decline from its higher percentages just after the Second World War), it is now a major force in French politics, one of roughly four equal Parties in the Republic. It is emerging from its excommunication during the years of the Fourth Republic and its eclipse during what, for it, must have been the long night of Gaullism. And, perhaps most significantly, the principal resistance of the Socialists to 'left unity' (a settled feature of the years 1947 to 1970) seems to have melted away.

Also, the Communist phenomenon is present today throughout the whole of Latin Europe, including Iberia. Although both of the Iberian Communist parties still lag far behind their respective Socialist and Social Democratic parties in votes, they have secured a greater measure of influence than their non-Communist adversaries in the trade unions. In Spain, the ideological and organization changes within the PCE, together with its highly flexible alliance policy, makes it a serious contender for political influence, if not power. Nor should the small but potent Portuguese Communist party be consigned by observers to permanent opposition. It retains a significant electoral constituency and an even more substantial trade union base.

Communist Parties remain an insignificant electoral force within the main Northern European nations, and are virtually absent altogether in West Germany. Yet in Britain, the still very small Communist party has in recent years made some important gains inside the powerful trade union movement, and is becoming increasingly acceptable to Labour's left-wing. The CPGB is more influential within key sectors of British trade union life than at any time since the Second World War.

These examples of the growth of Communism in Western Europe are complemented by a *sense* of expansion and movement, if not inevitability, which the arrival of 'Eurocommunism' has evinced. This *sense* of growth has been enhanced by the extensive media coverage of the Latin Communist parties, which often appears to concentrate upon the 'celebrity' status of the various Communist leaders. The Italian and Spanish Parties, in particular, seem to excite intellectuals throughout the West. Moreover, Communist Parties are increasingly acceptable to the democratic left in Europe in a way that the Communists of the fifties and sixties were not.

This *sense* of Communist Party advance is further underlined by the changed international and political climate. The Communist Parties of Italy and France were powerful contenders for power in the period just after the Second World War. But today, there seems little prospect of a repeat of the late forties—of a general West European and American cultural, political, intellectual and military reaction against the Communists. In short, because of the Communists' more careful tactics and the current decline of anti-Communism in the West, the Communist parties of France and Italy may have even more potential for growth and power than they had in the period 1945–8.

Even so, the facts and figures, which follow, about the development of Communism in Western Europe should be set in the context of the still powerful and often underrated democratic, political traditions of post-war Europe. The resilience and staying-power of the democratic forces in Western Europe may be open to question, but should not be underestimated. Even if Communist parties should embark upon a share of governmental power, or should even achieve it on their own (a prospect that seems decidedly dim), they will have great difficulty in attempting to 'transform' the nations of Western Europe into 'socialist' Communist states. In the two countries most immediately vulnerable, Italy and France, a strong 'bourgeois' class still remains, as does considerable antipathy towards the Communists on the part of millions of working-class people. The historic, social memory of liberal democracy and Western freedom will not readily be expunged; and if the Communists move too quickly to transform their societies, they will meet with powerful centres, majority centres, of resistance. Furthermore, although experiencing difficulties, the economies of Western Europe (including France and Italy) are not for the moment at least, nearly so fragile as to suggest a disintegration in the social order that could lead to revolutionary, political change. Also, a United States economic, military and political presence in Europe, together with a continuing and powerful West Germany, will inevitably put some kind of a brake on the development of Communism in Southern Europe.

The European Parties face formidable obstacles before they can radically 'transform' their societies. In the short run their power will continue to be limited, in spite of their participation in government, by the powerful democratic traditions, institutions, parties, habits and cultures of the nations they seek to 'transform'. If they should attempt to move too fast, a reaction could set in that could consign them to the sidelines again. If they move too slowly, they could split as resistance may build up from within the Communist Parties to their compromises and timidity.

In conclusion, Communism in Western Europe remains a minority phenomenon, but one with potential for further advance. It still has a long way to travel; but has reason to travel hopefully as it measures the success it has already achieved and the power it has already accrued.

Communists do not measure their own political power within a society exclusively in electoral terms. Communist Parties operate across a broad front. As well as attempting to make headway within the institutions of the democratic state (governments, legislatures), Communist Parties also attempt to secure change more generally within the political culture. This involves attempting to secure heightened 'class consciousness' by industrial action, such as influencing trade union movements and, depending upon the circumstances, either instigating strikes and industrial dislocation or by damping down workers' demands and playing the role of the 'responsible' party. Also, Communist Parties are keen to secure change in the intellectual climate through control of key sectors of the media and educational institutions, a strategy often described as 'building an ideological majority'.

A prerequisite for changing society across such a wide front remains a dedicated and disciplined party membership.

COMMUNIST PARTY MEMBERSHIP

Raw numbers of party members need not tell us much about the real strength of a Communist party in a total political system, although a sizeable membership rarely coincides with negligible political power. The Communist parties of Western Europe can, broadly speaking, be divided into two types: 'mass' parties and 'minor' parties (sometimes referred to as 'parties of militants' or 'vanguard parties').[6] The Italian Communist Party (PCI) is the archetypical 'mass' party with a large parliamentary representation, whereas the Communist Party of Great Britain (CPGB) represents a minor party with a significant influence in the industrial sector. Yet, to attempt to assess the strategic political power of either of these parties by reference simply to their membership totals could distort the picture. The PCI's membership figures, taken over a twenty-five year period, have fallen by about 1 million,[7] yet, their political power during that period has grown steadily. The CPGB's membership has been hovering round the 30,000 mark for several years, but its influence in key sectors of organized labour has grown since the middle sixties. Consequently, there is no necessary correlation between fluctuations in membership size and political power.

Even so, it remains the case that parties with large memberships are also the ones nearest to political power. Obviously, the larger the membership (as long as it is disciplined and committed) the greater the chance the CP has of permeating society, getting out the vote, and generally establishing itself as a political force to be reckoned with. To establish with accuracy the exact state of CP membership (as is true with all other parties) is a hazardous exercise. Scholars, and other interested observers, must ultimately rely upon information supplied to them by the Communist Parties themselves. By far the largest Western European Communist Party is the PCI. It claimed 1,794,008 party members in 1976 (over 3% of the total population). Furthermore, the PCI announced in the summer of 1977 that its 1977 membership had already reached its 1976 (September) levels. PCI membership has been on a steadily-rising curve since 1972,[8] reversing the downward trend of recent decades. In fact, it has been estimated that between 1971 and 1976 PCI membership has risen 18% more than the Italian population as a whole.

Figures for the French Communist Party (PCF) vary according to source, but a generally agreed figure seems to be somewhere in the region of 600,000. The PCF has virtually doubled its membership since the early 1960s, and in the last year appears to have continued to maintain this upward progression.[9] The only other Western European CPs which, arguably, even approach 'mass' status are the Portuguese (PCP) and the Spanish (PCE). Exact figures for the Iberian Parties are even more problematical than for the PCI or PCF because both parties are emerging from a period of clandestine operations. The PCP has an estimated membership of over 100,000; and Rui Machete suggests that the Party has recently engaged in a recruiting campaign which has pushed this number higher. Estimates of the membership of the PCE vary from 50,000 to 100,000 members[10] (the latter figure representing 0.2% of the population). All the other Western European Communist parties have negligible memberships.[11]

Set, then, in a pan-Western European perspective, these membership figures illustrate how relatively small the European Communist phenomenon still is when compared with the non-Communist parties (the parties of Conservatism, Liberalism, Christian and Social Democracy and Socialism taken together). Outside of France and Italy, by comparison with their 'bourgeois' competitors, they appear minute. Yet, the strength of the Communist movement lies partly in the disciplined and committed nature of its membership—of the whole party acting as one. This feature of Communist support probably ensures that some of the smaller parties are more significant than they seem on paper and certainly, as far as the 'mass' Latin parties are concerned, that the PCI and the PCF (and, arguably, too, the PCP) are the most powerfully organized political forces in their respective countries. It is impossible to assess, however, the relationship between the crude membership figures of the 'mass' parties and the number of 'cadres' or 'militants' within the ranks. Not every CP member is active, for many (particularly in Italy) enlist simply as insurance for the future.

The 'mass' parties, as they grow in numbers, obviously have a declining ratio of 'militants' to members. Interestingly, though, this does not apparently increase factionalism or cause serious disciplinary problems. The splits and public controversies

that have been a feature of some of the smaller parties (particularly the Greek and the British) have not generally been repeated
in the 'mass' parties. The psychological predeliction of new
members and the disciplinary apparatus apparently ensures
conformity, if not deep involvement, from 'non-active' members.

As they grow, the 'mass' parties tend to increase their turnover
rate, that is, the number of members leaving the Party and
being replaced by new recruits. In 1974, the PCF took a decision
to open up party membership to anyone desiring 'democratic
change', and this accelerated the entry of new members. Even
before then, however, the turnover rate in the French Party
had been significant. One student of Communism in Western
Europe has estimated that in the first few years of the seventies,
as much as 50% of the membership of the PCF 'turned over'.[12]
Since 1974, the 'turnover' rate may even have increased.
McInnes describes these fluctuations as representing 'an extra-
ordinary degree of instability for a political party'.[13] A hard
core of party regulars remain but, even so, the extent to which
the PCF has maintained unity and discipline in this fluctuating
party environment remains an intriguing feature of modern
European Communist life. The PCI, too, has a significant turn-
over rate, although it is considerably lower than that of the
PCF. Between 1972 and 1976, it has averaged 4.5% of over-all
party membership.

How have these fluctuations in membership within the 'mass'
parties affected their class, age, sex, regional and religious composition? And what is the significance of these changes for
the future?

Class: Both the PCI and the PCF remain predominantly working-class parties. In 1973, the percentage of PCI members who
were proletarian (that is, employed manual workers in the
industrial and agricultural sectors) was as high as 77.36. This
figure changed little from that of 1971. The figure for the
PCF, at the latest count, was 60.1%.[14]

In Italy, this proletarian category excludes both the peasants
and the middle class; and there have been noticeable developments in both these classes. Between 1971 and 1973, peasant
membership of the PCI fell by over 2.5%, whereas middle
class membership, as a percentage of the total, rose by over
2.5%. Professor Are has noticed another intriguing pattern.

He suggests that the middle-class tends to flock into the PCI in progressively larger and larger numbers the further it is from the more prosperous industrial and European areas of Italy, and the closer it is to the poorer areas afflicted by greater economic and social distortions. Whereas the percentage of PCI members who are middle class, rose between 1971 and 1973 by 1.3% in the Italian northern region, it rose by almost 2% in the central region and by a sizeable 6.6% in the south and 6.0% in the islands. Professor Are concludes from this data that the flow of sections of the middle class into the PCI members who are middle class, rose between 1971 and security, and the crumbling of their traditional cultural reference points—a process developing, but less quickly, in the north. Of course, there are also a number of middle class people who, no matter what their economic status and security, want to be on the winning side. There is some, fragmentary, evidence that this kind of increase in PCI middle class membership has gathered apace since 1974.

Evidence about the middle class that flows into the PCF is difficult to come by. Certainly, the PCF has attempted to attract into its ranks disaffected white-collar workers. Certainly, there was, as Kriegel has pointed out, a massive shift in the composition of Communist candidates from workers to teachers in the Seine region between 1924 and 1966.[15] McInnes suggests that: 'It has continued since then, and on a national basis.'[16]

What this accretion of middle class membership to still largely proletarian parties augurs for the future is debatable. The changes are still relatively small; but if the trend continues, it could give the PCI and the PCF a degree more establishment legitimacy and articulateness, even though their continued claims to be parties of the workers would look increasingly threadbare.[17] Disaffected middle class recruits could also add that edge of embittered resolution was so much a feature of revolutionary forces in Europe in the interwar period.

Age: The image Communist parties generally present to the outside world is that of an aging class-based male party, often reliving the past conflicts of the interwar period, particularly, the Spanish Civil War, hidebound by doctrine and Leninist procedure and uninterested in the romanticism and idealism

of youth. Certainly, in the fifties and sixties, this stereotype
of CP membership, even in the mass parties, was congruent
with reality. The CPs had aged. Both the PCF and the PCI
have attempted, particularly since the 1968 student revolts and
the growth of young ultra-left movements, to reverse this process.
The PCF seems, of the two, to have had most success. The
average age of its membership is declining.[18] On the other
hand, the PCI's age structure appears to have changed little
over recent years. The Party tends to gloss over the age distribution of its members while projecting itself as a young party.
One sign of this continuing problem in attracting young people
into the Party is the falling membership of its Federation of
Communist Youth (down 15% between 1976 and 1977). It
has been calculated that only 11% of PCI members are in
the age group 'under 25'.

The 'mass' CPs are certainly renewing themselves adequately
enough, although not as dramatically as they often claim. There
is no evidence that CP recruitment among the young is so
disastrous as to foretell a rapid decline in membership. One
political problem for the CPs seems, at the moment, intractable,
however: how to woo away from the ultra-left the politically
conscious young generation of Marxist activists. (No doubt,
if the 'mass' CPs continue to offer their members prospects
for promotion within their societies, a sufficient number of
these young activists, as they mature, will settle for the 'Eurocommunist' option in a mellowing process like that exhibited
by large numbers of American university radicals of the 1960s,
many of whom have entered the mainstream of American life.)
Another potential problem for the 'mass' parties will be their
ability to marshall coming younger generations into their disciplined party apparatus. Recent PCI problems with their youth
federations may herald larger difficulties in the future.

Sex: As with the youth issue, Communist parties have attempted
to eradicate their image as predominantly male parties. The
CPGB has attempted to link 'women's liberation' to the 'building of socialism' and see women's problems in terms of 'subjugation in their *personal* relationships'.[19]

The PCI is rather more orthodox, setting the inferiority of
women 'in terms of work and in community life'.[20] The PCI
has had to walk something of a tightrope on women's issues.

It has campaigned for women's rights and mobilized support on issues of great concern to women—such as the referendum on divorce in 1974 and the campaign for the liberalization of the abortion laws in 1976. At the same time, it is careful not to alienate itself from the prevailing opinions of what it terms 'the Catholic masses', particularly regarding the sanctity of family life. For instance, Berlinguer assailed 'libertarian theories' as 'drugs . . . that dissolve and dissipate . . . every authentic and family relationship'.[21]

There is little evidence, however, to show any dramatic increase in the number of women entering into membership of the 'mass' parties (or for that matter, the 'minor' parties either). In the PCI, the proportion of women members has remained relatively static over the last five years, at around 23%. Kriegel reports an increase in the percentage of female membership of the PCF between 1966 and 1972 (up from 25.5% to 30%).[22] Communist parties remain overwhelmingly male, as do most other left parties in Europe. There is no Communist equivalent to the mass involvement of women activists which is a feature, particularly, of the British Conservative Party.

Regions: Area, provincial and regional patterns of Communist membership within the West European nations are too varied to produce any sensible theories other than the most general. In the major Northern European nations, Britain and West Germany, CP membership is heavily concentrated in the industrial regions where trade union solidarity is strongest. The DKP draws the vast majority of its members from the industrial and mining regions of the Ruhr. The CPGB's membership is heavily concentrated in the older, decaying, industrial regions of Scotland, the East End of London, South Wales and Lancashire.[23] Communist membership is virtually non-existent in the rural areas of Northern Europe where agriculture is highly mechanized and efficient, and there is no peasantry. In East Anglia, for instance, a large rural area with a history of radical Liberalism (and some Labour representation in Parliament), the CPGB can boast only 250 members.

In Latin Europe, scholars have adumbrated two types of Communist support—an industrial, urban, proletarian kind, growing out of a socialist and social-democratic working-class tradition; and a rural, peasant Communism, frequently less

ideological and class-conscious, rooted instead in protest about
social conditions and in anti-clericalism. Of course, the former
is larger than the latter throughout Latin Europe, but both
decidedly exist. Although the PCP is primarily a workers' party
with most of its membership concentrated in the industrial
areas of Lisbon (and, to a lesser extent, in Oporto), it can
claim considerable strength among the farm labourers of Alentejo, south and east of Lisbon.[24] PCE support among the Spanish
peasantry is less impressive. It attracts little support from the
peasants proper—those with small holdings (or *minifundia*).
There is not much more from the rural proletariat of the
great estates or *latifundia*. In regional terms, the PCE's membership is largely concentrated in Madrid, Barcelona and the Cata-
lonian provinces, the Asturias mining region, and parts of Andalusia. Both the PCF and the PCI are much more broadly
based in terms of regional and sector membership. PCF strength,
although centred round the industrial regions of Northern
France, is also substantial among the peasants of the Massif
Central and, particularly, in the Rhone region.[25] The regional
and sector spread of PCI membership is more even than the
continuing, though diminishing, economic and social differences
between the various regions would suggest.

Professor Are, for this study, has analyzed the PCI member/in-
habitant ratio of all the regions of Italy, and his conclusions
about the geographical spread of Communist membership show
how all-pervasive this, the most important European Communist
Party, has become within the total society. In the 'Red Belt'
of Central Italy in Emilia-Romagna, Tuscany and Umbria,
the Party member/inhabitant ratio is, respectively, 1 to 9, 1
to 14 and 1 to 18 (the national average being 1 to 33). In
the north-west, in the regions of Piedmont, Liguria and Lombardy, it is, respectively 1 to 51, 1 to 24 and 1 to 44. In
the heavily Catholic north east and the 'white regions' of
Veneto, Trentino–Alto Adige and Friuli–Venezia–Giulia, it is,
respectively, 1 to 53, 1 to 175 and 1 to 50. In the Marche
region of central Italy, it is 1 to 25 and in the Lazio region,
which includes Rome, it is 1 to 51. In the very extensive
group of regions comprising the Italian south, the ratio is 1
to 54 inhabitants.

This member/inhabitant ratio provides an important yardstick
for measuring the extent of PCI presence in society generally:

and, significantly, it has improved in all the regions since 1970. Also, although there are significant disparities between regions, these appear to be narrowing. As with the PCI vote, the member/inhabitant ratio has become more uniform throughout the country. Although, as we have seen earlier, the percentage of peasants in membership fell between 1971 and 1973, the fact that the PCI can continue to secure such a high member/inhabitant ratio in regions like Romagna and Umbria (containing large rural pockets), and has built up membership in the South virtually from scratch, shows the continuing wide social spread of its support. This increasingly 'all-pervasive' geographic spread of PCI support is the single most important feature that distinguishes the PCI from all other major Western Communist Parties.

Religion: There is a paucity of research in all the Southern European countries on the relationship of Communist Party membership to the Catholic Church; on whether there is any changing relationship between Catholic belief and CP membership; on whether the decline in the power of the Church has affected CP membership; on whether the results of the second Vatican Council in 1964 have had any political effects; and on whether the growth of social and left Catholicism has affected Communist membership and support. Certainly, the various Latin Communist parties have courted the working class Catholic vote and have sought to ease relations with the Church. As early as 1956, the underground PCE started to encourage Communist–Catholic contacts, and Dolores Ibarruri declared membership of the Party open to priests.[26] Carrillo, too, has stressed the need for the PCE to win over the Church if it is to emerge victorious.[27]

In France, Roger Garaudy, the PCF's house philosopher until his expulsion in 1969, courted left Catholicism. McInnes points out that the PCF establishment preferred, rather, to deal with non-political Catholic leaders—there were more votes to be gained that way.[28] In Italy, the PCI, in its social policy and moral posture, steers clear of offending the Church (indeed, Signora Berlinguer goes to Mass, often with attendant publicity); it encourages that section of the Vatican hierarchy which desires a Concordat-style settlement (separate spheres of influence) with the PCI; and it attempts to involve Communists in joint endeavours (public meetings, protests) with Catholics on *ad hoc* issues as they arise.

What all these overtures have achieved for the Communist parties is obscure. They seem, mainly, to have been aimed at easing the general political environment for the CPs and at attracting votes. It is unlikely that the Communist parties, with the possible exception of the PCE, would want to attract into their organized rank and file practising, devout Catholics. To accept the votes of the Catholic masses is one thing; to welcome practising Catholics into the body of the party is, decidedly, another.

COMMUNISTS AT THE POLLS

Any survey of Communist party voting strength should contain two qualifications as to its relevance. First, electoral support is an important, though not conclusive, guide to Communist Party power within a society. The case of Britain is instructive. In its 57-year history, the CPGB has managed to obtain only two Members of Parliament, and the House of Commons has been without CP representation since 1950. The party managed to poll a paltry 17,008 votes in the general election of October, 1974—less than its own claimed membership,[29] and less, too, than the votes accrued by its extremist counterpart on the right, the small neo-fascist National Front. In the October, 1974 election, the CPGB was expected to do best in the Dunbartonshire Central division of Scotland. This Clydeside area has a history of Communist industrial militancy and does not view the CP with as much innate suspicion and antagonism as do other regions of the UK. It is the heart of the 'red Clyde' region. The result was revealing: Labour, 40.2%; Scottish National Party, 29.1%; Conservatives, 17.2%; Communists, 8.7%; Liberals, 4.8%.[30]

Secondly, just as a Communist party should not be underestimated by its poor, indeed negligible, showing at the polls, neither should good electoral results be misinterpreted as a mandate for Communism. Not all CP voters are Communists; some are not even Communist sympathizers. Votes cast for Communist candidates may measure protest against an existing government as much as Communist commitment or sympathy. Where Communist candidates are second in constituencies (as is often the case after the first round of voting in France), or where the Communist party is second nationally (as in Italy), voting Communist may be the most effective method of opposing, limiting, or simply frightening the majority party.

Also, apart from the hard core of habitual Communist voters, there is evidence that many of those who vote Communist do so for 'instrumental' reasons. They see the Communist party, like any other, as an 'instrument' to achieve certain objectives (usually economic). Such support, it is believed, can be withdrawn again in the future if the party does not live up to expectations. In other words, the Communist Party is seen by many voters (particularly in Latin Europe) as qualitatively similar to the democratic parties—as a political convenience to be supported or opposed, according to circumstances. Some political scientists have argued that 'instrumental' voting is increasing,[31] particularly amongst affluent workers. If this is the case, it would be arbitrary to exclude the CPs as electoral repositories for this tendency.

Even so, although voting Communist in a secret ballot entails no long term commitment to the cause, it does denote a certain acceptability, a lack on the part of the voter of traditional suspicions or fears. Therefore, the size of the Communist vote in Western Europe need not tell us the size of Communist commitment (CP membership is a better guide to that); it can tell us, however, the degree of acceptability that the Party has won, the amount by which it has overcome traditional hostility and its potential for the future.

If we divide Western Europe (roughly) into north and south, then a striking divergence in the acceptability of the Communists can be noted. In Northern Europe, at the most recent general elections, the CPs gained an average per nation of 5.01% of the vote. These figures, of course, are distorted upwards by the large number of small countries (such as Norway, Iceland and Luxembourg) where the CP gained a relatively large share of the vote.[32] In the four Latin countries of Southern Europe (Portugal, Spain, France and Italy), the average per nation is approximately 20%. Taking these four Latin countries as a whole, the size of the Communist vote in the most recent national elections was 20.3 million.[33] This compares with the 17.2 million votes cast for Socialist and Social Democratic parties.[34] Clearly, if one looks at Southern Europe, the Communists have established themselves as the leading party of the left among the electorate. In each individual country, of course, the picture is rather different: the Communists are well behind the PSOE in Spain and the Socialists in Portugal, but only marginally behind the Socialists in France and significantly ahead of the nearest left party (by over 9 million votes for the Chamber of Deputies) in Italy.

Italy Italy is the great success story for Communist electoral politics. The PCI's vote at the general election of 1976 was 12,620,502, 34.44% of the total. Furthermore, except perhaps for 1948, the PCI's popular vote has risen consistently at every general election since the war:[35]

Year	PCI vote	% of total
June 1946	4,356,686	19.0
June 1953	6,120,809	22.6
May 1958	6,704,454	22.7
April 1963	7,763,854	25.3
May 1968	8,557,404	26.9
May 1972	9,085,927	27.2
June 1976	12,620,502	34.4

The story is of a steady, unremitting increase with a significant breakthrough (a remarkable jump of 39.15% in their vote between 1972 and 1976) in the seventies.

An interesting sidelight on PCI electoral advance is that it has been approximately in inverse relationship to Socialist and Social Democratic decline (the PSI's percentage of the vote has dropped from 21% in 1946 to 9.66% in 1976). The PCI's share of the 'left' vote has soared from 47.7% in 1946 to 73.8% in 1976.

As we have seen, PCI membership also rose significantly (by 18.77%) between 1971 and 1976, but it would seem to be on less of a dramatically upturned curve than PCI votes. This could create problems for the PCI, as for the first time its votes are rising out of all proportion to its hard core, activist membership. PCI response to this gap has been to renew its fidelity to the tradition of 'the party of the masses' initiated by Palmiro Togliatti, its guiding spirit and leader for many decades. It still wants more members and campaigns to expand.

By this method, it attempts to ensure that, as the total vote grows, so does the hard core membership.

The social make up of the PCI electorate is difficult to measure for 1976. Even so, three successive sample inquiries (1968, 1972 and 1975) show some interesting trends. For instance, the percentage of PCI voters in manual jobs fell significantly between 1968 and 1975;[36] this tends to confirm that the PCI electorate is becoming more broadly based socially (a similar trend to that indicated within the PCI membership). In fact, the PCI electorate (socially) is beginning to resemble the Italian electorate as a whole, although it is still tilted somewhat towards an over-representation of manual workers. A striking fact of modern Italian electoral politics is that today both the Christian Democrats and the PCI can claim to be broadly based socially. This used to be the preserve of the Christian Democrats.[37]

Regionally, too, the PCI electorate is increasing its representative character. In 1976, the PCI's vote was more uniform throughout the nation than at any time in its history. Although the PCI vote rose in all regions, its percentage *increase* was less in the 'Red' areas than in many of the traditionally Christian Democratic or marginal areas. In 'Red' Romagna, Tuscany and Umbria, it rose (between 1972 and 1976) by 5.01%; whereas in the traditionally Christian Democratic South and Islands, it rose by 7.7%. Even in the very heartland of Christian Democracy (Veneto, Trentino, Alto Adige, the Friuli Venezia–Giulia) it rose by 6.2%.[38] The PCI is now either the leading or second party in all the significant regions in Italy. This wide geographic breakthrough means that the PCI can now, more easily, benefit from the 'instrumental' vote. It is the natural party for the non-partisan, discontented to vote for, if they wish to oust an existing local or national administration.

The power of the PCI in the various regions of Italy can be contrasted with that of the British Liberal Party in order to draw out the importance, for an opposition political party, of a regional base. The British Liberals achieved over 20% of the popular vote in the February, 1974 British general election yet they could only muster thirteen seats in Parliament. They were denied their much-heralded breakthrough because they could not establish themselves as the second Party in the country, nor indeed as the second Party in a region. The British Liberals, unlike the PCI, have no regional base.

The age, sex and religious breakdown of the PCI vote is more difficult to determine than the regional one. Significantly, more women (strikingly so in the South) continue to vote for the Christian Democrats than the PCI, although this gap is probably narrowing. The number of Catholics voting for the PCI is almost impossible to determine. Are suggests that religious observance has slumped today in Italy in all classes of society; and no research has yet been carried out into the connection between this development and political behaviour. It does not need an overly speculative mind, however, to conclude that PCI acceptability is likely to grow as religious commitment declines, or, alternatively, in the event of a philosophic convergence or political detente (between Catholicism and Communism). The PCI attracted 37.5% of the young (18–25 year old) vote in 1976. This was higher than the vote it attracted from Italians as a whole, and significantly, more impressive than the PCI's ability to attract (and keep) young Italians as party *members*.

France   The PCI, in terms of the spread of its social and regional support at the polls, can now fairly claim to be as much a national and representative party as the Christian Democrats. In this respect, the Italian Communists possess a political legitimacy within their nation that the PCF cannot match within France. The PCF has never achieved more than 28.6% of the popular vote in any general election since the war, and from this (November 1946) high point, it has slipped back to 20.6% in the first round in March, 1978. Its post-war average equals 23.4% of the vote, and at no election has it been 4.95% more or less than this figure. In fact, in the five Assembly elections since 1962, its vote has varied by only 2.5%. Unlike the PCI, it is on a very slightly undulating horizontal electoral curve. Consequently, for parliamentary election purposes, it is in need of major alliances.

The PCF has a wide geographic base in the sense that the Communist vote is not restricted to the northern industrial areas (it has a rural support, particularly where its membership is high—in the centre of France (Berry and Agenais) and in the Midi).[39] Yet the PCF lacks the PCI's all-pervasive geographical presence. In terms of social breakdown, about 50% of the PCF vote is working class and just under 10% peasant;[40] yet the PCF only manages to secure for its candidates between a quarter and a third of the total working-class vote. In fact, both the Socialists and the 'parties of the majority' can claim to be only slightly less working class in their appeal.[41]

A striking feature of the PCF electorate is its apparently growing appeal to wage earners in the public sector. It is from within this category that the PCF won more votes in 1973 than any other single party. This may help to explain the inordinate interest shown by the PCF in further nationalizations. In 1973, it had 33% of the votes of wage earners in the public sector, compared to 27% in the private sector. It would seem reasonable to believe that the PCF sees the expansion of the public sector as one way out of its present electoral impasse.

All in all, French Communism at the polls has been a static phenomenon, devoid of the sense of movement and permeation so much a feature of the Italian variety. Although the PCF can, at first reckoning, count on its habitual fifth of the voting electorate, the resistance to it from the remaining four-fifths seems to be a permanent fact of life. If the PCF wants to continue to tread the parliamentary road, it would seem that it has only two options available. First, it can seek to re-establish the alliance that it forged with the Socialists in 1972. This strategy presumes both a united Socialist Party and one willing to resurrect a Common Programme yet again, even after the traumas of the Socialist/Communist split in the autumn of 1977. Alternatively, the PCF can hope to be the beneficiary of a weak and fractured Socialist Party and of an economic crisis which may impel wavering voters towards radical economic solutions. In the short run, however, there seems little that the PCF can do to make itself a more attractive political force. It will continue to need alliances.

Iberia The Iberian peoples, after a long interregnum, are new to the experience of democratic elections. Consequently, the electoral patterns set since the overthrow of Caetano and the death of Franco may tell us little about the future. The PCE, in its first post-Franco test of public opinion, did not do as well as many observers had expected. Its 9.4% share of the

popular vote in the June, 1977 parliamentary elections produced
only 20 (out of 350) seats in the Chamber of Deputies. Its
vote was heavily concentrated in Catalonia, Andalusia and
Madrid. In the rest of Spain it remains a negligible electoral
force. It returned no deputies at all in Galicia, León, Estrema-
dura, Murcia, Old Castile, Navarre and Aragon nor, surpris-
ingly, in the Basque country. It returned only one deputy
from the mining region of the Asturias.[42]

The reasons for the relatively modest showing of the PCE
are dimly perceived by scholars and observers. Certainly, the
new electoral system in Spain over-represents the more conservative, rural parts of the country, and this would help account
for the discrepancy between the PCE's popular vote and its
parliamentary representation. Another suggestion is that the
PCE had little time, following its legalization, to prepare for
the election: even so, its highly organized machine should have
been able to overcome this particular obstacle. The answer
probably lies in part in the powerful electoral performance
of its main left competitors, the Socialists (PSOE), who achieved
28.5% of the popular vote. Even so, by garnering 1.7 million
votes, the PCE established itself as the third largest electoral
force in the country, incidentally, doing much better than it
did in the pre-Franco Republic when it last ran as a separate
party (before electoral merger into the Popular Front). The
political situation in Spain remains fluid. The PSOE is prone
to divisions, eclectic philosophically and its leadership untested;
Carrillo is shrewd, seasoned and subtle; the future of the PCE
as a powerful electoral force cannot be ruled out; but it will
need alliances.

Although the image (and reality) of the PCP is one of unreconstructed Stalinism, its electoral support is substantially greater
than that of the PCE and approaches that of the PCF. It
achieved (in alliance with its political front organization, the
Portuguese Democratic Movement) 17.65% of the vote in the
elections for the constituent assembly in April, 1975. Although
it received a setback in the Presidential election in June, 1976
(because of the competing left candidacy of Otelo Carvalho),
it returned to 17.7% in an electoral alliance with the Portuguese
Democratic Movement in the municipal election of December,
1976. Even so, rather like the PCF, the PCP seems, for the
moment, to be contained at this level.

Two points stand out from an analysis of Communism at the polls in Latin Europe. First, it remains a persistent minority political movement; at its highest point (in Italy in 1976) 65.5% of the electorate voted against it. Secondly, it is only in Italy that the Communist Party appears to have made a significant enough electoral breakthrough to be within sight of political power obtained through the ballot box. Even here, though, where electoral advance in the seventies has been swift, the PCI would seem to have the prospect of years of alliances and power-sharing as its most optimistic goal. An over-all majority for the PCI in the Italian Parliament still seems an unattainable goal for years to come. The other Latin parties, apart from the PCE, appear to be on a plateau of electoral support upwards from which they cannot jump. In this still largely hostile electoral environment, all the Southern European CPs will continue to work on a broad front—seeking societal-political power by other means as well as through the polls.

COMMUNIST PARTIES AND TRADE UNIONS

In measuring the extent of the Communist phenomenon, it is essential to take into account more than the Party's electoral strength and membership. Indeed, one of the major distinguishing characteristics of the Communist Party is its emphasis on utilizing other organizations to increase its strength. In this the Communist Party is unique. Democratic parties occasionally will try to gain control of and utilize other institutions, but they do not, and probably cannot, systematically seek to control and mobilize most of the major sectors of society. They do not possess either the inclination or the disciplined cadre to create a 'state within a state' and utilize such a 'machine' to consolidate their control over the entire society.

There is, of course, nothing basically new in this Communist strategy. However, some significant new elements are evident in the way the European parties implement this approach.

There are three basic arenas which the Communists seek to influence. First, they focus on obtaining significant influence in important non-governmental organizations, or what Communists call 'organizations of the masses'. In the United States and Great Britain these frequently are referred to as 'front organizations'.[43] These are voluntary organizations to which sizeable numbers of people belong and which are influential in modern society. The Communists cannot hope to incorporate all the members of these organizations into the Party. Indeed, even if they could, they would probably be reluctant to do so because it would be difficult to incorporate them without weakening Party discipline and diluting the ideology. Moreover, because the organizations are not officially Communist, either in objectives or membership, they can play a useful role as a non-Communist facade or 'front'—providing, of course, Communists are at the helm.

Communist direction comes about as a result of discreet penetration of these significant non-Communist organizations by Communist militants under the discipline of the Communist Party. In Europe, this type of penetration is often called *noyautage*. The Communist groups that operate in this fashion are called *noyaux* or fractions.[44]

The second arena of Communist activity is the institutions of the state. Lenin counselled Communist parties to destroy the apparatus of the state (the administration, the police, the army) immediately after seizing power, and replace it with new institutions under the control of the 'dictatorship of the proletariat.' However, this strategy has recently been replaced by a different approach, particularly in the Southern European parties.

Rather than wait for the revolution before neutralizing the bourgeois state, the Parties now seek to infiltrate its institutions so as to insure that they are not used to weaken the Party before and after the party becomes part of the government. Then, when the party wins full revolutionary power, the state institutions will not have to be destroyed, but merely purged of recalcitrant individuals. The British Communist Party has obligingly outlined in precise detail how such a purge might take place: 'Those who proved unwilling to implement government policy, or incapable of doing so, would be retired or found other jobs, while those who tried actively to sabotage the implementation of socialist legislation would be dealt with under the law.'[45] An exact interpretation of the precise meaning of 'sabotage' is not supplied.

The Communists apparently feel they can afford to allow their militants to work for the state without risking that they be co-opted or embrace bourgeois habits. Party cadres remain under strict party discipline. The CPs discovered through experience that they were able to control their Members of Parliament and elected municipal officials, as well as their cadres in front organizations, and they have concluded that this is a viable strategy in many of the non-elected institutions of the state.

The third area of Communist activity is in what Marx called the 'ideological superstructure' of society. Elaborated upon in the works of the Italian Communist theoretician, Antonio Gramsci (1891–1937), practiced by the PCI and PCE, and much discussed in France after the events of May 1968, the parties have come to emphasize the 'cultural' approach to winning power. By gaining influence in schools, portions of the clergy, the trade unions, the media, and major cultural vehicles, the parties believe that they will be able to create an ideological majority that will be even more important than their parliamentary majority—because, they believe, there are cultural pre-conditions for winning political power. As long as newspapers, television, sermons and schoolbooks reflect the existing situation of capitalist ownership and wide differences of wealth and power among classes, people accept it as normal and proper. However, if the message people receive at school, in the media and at church is that the present situation is deficient, and that change is to be expected, then the public will no longer passively accept the capitalist order. Such a change in public attitudes is essential if revolutionary political action is to have major effects, said Gramsci. Consequently, the European parties now place even greater emphasis than heretofore, on intellectuals and the media in an effort to augment Communist strength.[46]

Information on the parties' influence in front organizations, governmental institutions (such as the police, military and civil service) and the cultural arena is very difficult to come by. It is easy, of course, to exaggerate Communist influence in these arenas and to demonstrate that the Communists pose a major threat. Yet, it is also easy to minimize the extent of Communist control, and suggest that the parties not only do not control significant institutions, but are in fact being co-opted by them. Unfortunately, there have been few systematic scholarly studies of these subjects, even on a country-by-country basis.[47]

Trade Unions However, in one of the most important non-governmental organizations, the trade unions, it is possible to estimate Communist strength. In most of southern Europe, as well as in Britain (but not in most of northern Europe), the Communist parties control sizeable sections of the labour movement. While many of the workers in the Communist-controlled unions of southern Europe are not members of the party, do not vote Communist, and cannot be relied upon to follow party policy automatically (unless they believe it is coincidental with their own interests), Communist strength in organized labour adds an important dimension to Communist power in Europe. It enables a Communist party to exploit issues with force and to achieve an influence beyond that which could be exerted simply through party membership alone.

Based on an examination of the political identity of the leadership, the domestic and foreign policy of the trade unions and what is known about their sources of financial support, it would appear that Communist parties have been able to take control of sizeable front organizations.[48]

In France, Italy and Portugal, over half the trade union movement is led by Communists; in Spain it is about 40%. In France and Italy, there are three national centres, but in both countries the leaders of the major centres, the CGT in France and the CGIL in Italy, are Communist. In France, for example, nine of the twelve members of the CGT top decision-making body are leaders of the Communist Party (two are in the Politburo and several are on the Central Committee of the PCF); and in Italy, the majority faction of the leadership group of the CGIL are CP members, several of them high ranking. In Spain, approximately 40% of the delegates elected in the first major trade union elections in over forty years (spring, 1978) were candidates of the Communist confederation (the Trade Union Confederation of the Workers' Commissions). Twenty-four out of 27 members of the top policy-making body of the Commissions, the *Coordinadora General*, are members of the PCE. Of these, two are on the Executive Committee of the Party and nearly half are members of the PCE's Central Committee. In Portugal, approximately 287 out of 360 unions (91% of the workers affiliated to trade unions) in the country belong to or work closely with the CGTP-IN (or Intersindical) which is controlled by the PCP.

The domestic and foreign policy positions of these Communist-led unions are also almost identical with the positions of their respective Communist Parties. Although there have been occasional divergencies, usually on relatively minor issues, the Communist Parties for years have been able to have their views on major issues adopted by the union bureaucracy.

In their over-all foreign policy positions, the unions identify completely with their respective Communist Parties. Although foreign affairs is not the major concern of unions and their press, the CGT, CGIL, Intersindical (in Portugal) and, in general, the Spanish Workers' Commissions, support the foreign policy aims of their respective Communist Parties. Usually they lend their weight to whatever issue their Party and Moscow are promoting at any given time, (for example, anti-neutron bomb, pro-Ethiopia, and pro-PLO campaigns). They almost always praise life, and the conditions of workers, in the Soviet bloc and condemn US foreign policy and the activities of other 'imperialist' forces.

On the international trade union level, they follow the general line adopted by their Party, and generally co-operate with Soviet-controlled international labour bodies such as the World Federation of Trade Unions (WFTU). Equally, when for tactical domestic reasons the Parties wish to distance themselves from Moscow, and attempt to enter into the mainstream of European politics, the trade unions follow suit. For example, in line with PCI international posture, the CGIL in the mid 1970s dropped its affiliated status with the WFTU and became an associate member, largely so that it could join the non-Communist European Trade Union Confederation (the pan-European labour body representing unions in the EEC). In the same way, the Spanish Workers' Commissions and the Portuguese Intersindical have not become affiliated to the WFTU, so that they, too, will have the flexibility to enter into non-Communist international labour bodies. This posture is consistent with Moscow's long-term drive for the reunification of the international labour movement under its own auspices. These trade union organizations of course remain very much involved in Soviet labour bloc activities. They fraternize and exchange innumerable delegations with Soviet bloc labour officials and the WFTU, as well as with each other.

What little is known about the financial relationships between the parties and their unions indicates that there is a close relationship between them. In France, the CGT has for years received considerable support from both the PCF and the Soviet bloc. This was documented shortly after the Second World War by the then Minister of the Interior, the Socialist Party leader Jules Moch. Since that time Jean Montaldo, in the most comprehensive study published of a party's finances, points out that the funds of the major front organizations, including the CGT, are deposited in a Soviet-owned bank, where the PCF also deposits its money.[49] The French journals *Est et Ouest* and *Les Etudes Sociales et Syndicales* have also analyzed the CGT's and the PCF's financial structure and have concluded that internally derived CGT resources, while considerable, are not sufficient to account for all its activities. Almost certainly the CGT is receiving funding from external sources, from the PCF or the Soviets or both.

Less is known about the financial relations of the Italian and Spanish unions. In the past it was generally believed that the Russians and the PCI contributed to the CGIL. Since the establishment of a type of check off system, and for other reasons, however, the unions in Italy have become much more financially independent. Indeed, one of the few analyses of the PCI's finances contends that the CGIL is 'now a major contributor to PCI coffers'[50] which, if true, is an indication of an encounter of a very intimate kind.

The Spanish Party and its underground trade union apparatus have undoubtedly received Soviet support over the years. More recently, it is believed that the Workers' Commissions received support from the WFTU and some Eastern European unions and sympathetic West European unions such as the CGT and CGIL.[51]

In Portugal, however, it is fairly clear that the PCP's unions have received considerable financial support from both the party itself and from the Soviet bloc.[52] Furthermore, both former Prime Minister Harold Wilson and former Secretary of State Henry Kissinger have made separate public estimates of Soviet financial transfers to Portuguese Communists which vary between $50 and $100 million.[53]

Based on the overlapping leadership, in addition to financial support, and the apparent subservience of the unions on policy questions, it would appear that the southern European Parties control approximately half of the trade union movement in their respective countries. Some, of course, would maintain that this has only limited utility. They would point out that approximately only one quarter to one third of all the workers in these countries are organized, that the labour movement is not powerful in southern Europe, and that it is the unions which influence the Parties, and not the other way round.[54]

While it is correct to suggest that most workers in Europe are not members of unions, this is true of most industrial nations. Indeed, outside Scandanavia the southern European pattern is not unusual. In the US, for example, even less than one quarter of the workers are union members; yet, few would deny that the AFL–CIO is one of the most important centres of power in the country. In addition to the union's political apparatus, union members have families which vote and union members themselves are inclined to vote and be more politically active than non-union members.

It is true, of course, that most southern European unions tend to be weaker and more divided in the workplace and in the bargaining process than, for example, American unions. However, as regards political activities, the Europeans frequently have resources, organizational technology and machinery that outstrips the political capacity of American unions, although, unlike the American labour movement, they rarely can utilize this machinery independently of the political party they are tied to.

Finally, while it is possible that the demands of the non-Communist workers are relayed back to the Communist party leaders, and Communist union officials, in an effort to maintain their union position, may come to represent their members to the Communist party, this has not appeared to be the predominant pattern. Rarely have the unions even debated a policy, come to a decision and secured its adoption by the party. Almost always it is the other way around. This, of course, is not surprising. Communist union officials, like other Communist officials, maintain their position by virtue of the support they receive from the party machinery. If the party leadership, including the union leaders in the Politburo or Executive Committee, decides to replace a given Communist trade union official or transfer him to other work, this can be engineered quite easily. Individuals serve the party first, and their organization second.

This is not to say that the party will ignore the advice

of its union leaders and specialists on trade union affairs. Indeed, the views of the CGT leader, Georges Seguy, or the CGIL leader, Luciano Lama, are probably among the most decisive in the party decision process. But once the top leadership decides what is best for the party, the union bureaucracy falls into line.

The ability of the party to control the wider union membership, however, is not so clear-cut. A great deal depends on the specific issues involved and on whether the non-Communist unions are well organized and can pose an effective counterweight to the Communists. It also depends on whether all the officials in the Communist unions from the top through the intermediate ranks down to the local level are members of the party. If they are, as is the case in many big plants in France and Italy, for example, then they will be in a position to influence the membership. If they are not, it will be more difficult for the party to transmit its directives into action.

Even if 90% of the local officials are party members, it is not always easy for the party to control the union's rank and file. After the Second World War, for example, workers in France and Italy rebelled against the parties' and the CGT's and CGIL's 'Stakhanovite' policy,[55] as well as their attempt to wreck the Marshall Plan in 1947 and 1948. Much more recently, many Italian workers have been uneasy with the PCI's and CGIL's moderate wage demands. Communist union leaders are usually keenly aware, however, of the potential and real contradictions between the economic needs and demands of trade union members on the one hand, and the use of trade union power for political purposes on the other. Sometimes this contradiction can cause the CPs severe problems of political and industrial management.

Nevertheless, control of the union machinery (through thousands of full time shop stewards and the labour press) enables the party to reach millions of workers on a daily basis (approximately 5 million union members and several million non-dues-paying but sympathetic workers in southern Europe). Moreover, the parties have and continue to use the union machinery to mobilize workers for demonstrations and electoral activity. This enables them to organize massive demonstrations, short political strikes, and other activities that can influence non-Communist voters and politicians. It gives the party a leverage that is out of all proportion to the number of Communists in the workers' ranks.

The extent to which the party can use its union strength and machinery in moments of political crisis (for instance, in order to help, or prevent, a coup) is difficult to assess. Yet, the history of the twentieth century is replete with examples of the strategic importance of trade union power, both as a mechanism for attempts at seizing power or for creating instability.[56]

In Britain, the trade union movement is equally, if not more important—but in several different ways. Britain, of the major industrial nations, is the most highly unionized. Over 10 million members, almost half the work force, belong to trade unions. In addition, most of the unions are directly affiliated to one of the major political parties, and are the most important single interest group which the British government has to take into account. Although completely impotent electorally, the CPGB, at least until very recently, has achieved a significant measure of influence in the industrial, and to some extent in the political, arena through its strength in the trade union movement.

CPGB strategy in the trade unions exists on two levels. First, there is a political strategy aimed at influencing the direction of the Labour Party. At the last count there were 62 trade unions (including almost every major union) directly affiliated to the Labour Party. These unions control over 80% of the votes cast at the Annual Conference of the Labour Party and elect (directly or indirectly) 18 out of the 28 members of Labour's National Executive Committee (the governing body of the party between Annual Conferences). The Annual Conference and the National Executive Committee determine over-all party policy and, together with the local constituency Labour parties, select the Labour candidates for Parliament.

Secondly, there is the CPGB's industrial strategy aimed at influencing the trade unions in their industrial role. British governments consult the TUC leaders, both formally and informally, over a wide range of policies before they are presented to Parliament. Trade union power in Britain, publicly enhanced after the defeat of the Heath Government by the miners in 1973/4, was codified by a series of 'Social Contracts' between the Labour government and the TUC, the intent of which is still in force at the time of writing. Consequently, control of, or influence within, the trade union movement can lead to a political voice in the direction of British society, irrespective of the power that voice has electorally.

In the internal British political debate, the question is even now raised as to whether a new administration will be able to govern Britain effectively if it does not agree with trade union economic and social priorities. Mrs Margaret Thatcher, the leader of the Conservative Party, at the 1977 Conservative Conference, stated, in her speech: 'The key question I am asked over and over again is ... "Will the trade unions allow a Conservative government to govern? ...."'[57]

For most of its life, the British trade union movement has been under the control of social democrats. This was certainly the case in the post-war years and remained the case well into the middle 1960s. The trade union leaders were the principal backers of Hugh Gaitskell, the ardently social democratic leader of the Labour Party from 1956 to 1963. Yet, as the sixties progressed, the political complexion of the major trade unions began to change. In many unions the social democratic leadership was succeeded by left socialists. This trend was described by Lord George-Brown, former deputy Leader of the Labour Party and Foreign Secretary, in April, 1972: 'In the fifties and sixties the men at the head of the unions were genuine social democrats ... Now, I think today that the situation is different. The major unions are the subject of a different kind of leadership, with a different outlook'.[58]

For the most part this 'different kind of leadership' was left socialist—democratic socialist, as opposed to Social Democrat. The left socialist tradition in Britain, unlike on the Continent, was until recently based upon utopian, Christian and co-operative ideas. Frank Cousins, the General Secretary of the Transport and General Union from the mid fifties to the mid sixties was in this tradition. More recently, however, the left in the Labour Party and unions has displayed a decidedly more Marxist complexion.

During the fifties, sixties and early seventies, the CPGB has been concentrating upon penetrating some of the key unions, and its efforts have not been in vain. Approximately 40 out of the 350 most important trade union officers are members of the Communist Party. Britain's giant Transport and General Workers' Union is one of the most deeply penetrated unions.

Although the executive does not play as significant a role as is the case in most other unions, of its 39 members at least a quarter are open members of the CPGB. The second largest union, the Amalgamated Union of Engineering Workers, has been the arena for a battle royal between the CPGB and moderate forces. Control shifts back and forth, but the Communists have certainly established a powerful presence within its governing councils. Recent elections in the AUEW, culminating in the victory of the avowedly anti-Communist Terry Duffy as President (to succeed Hugh Scanlon), represents a major setback for the Communist Party. This, together with the defeat of Communist Les Dixon for the AUEW Executive, may be a harbinger of things to come.

The powerful Miners' Union, on the other hand, still has a large CPGB contingent within its central leadership. Its Vice-President, and President of the Scottish Miners' Union, is Mick McGahey, President of the CPGB itself. Most of the other important unions, with the exception of the Electricians (who still bar Communists from holding office) and the General and Municipal Union, have Communists in various positions of authority.

There is no single union of which the CPGB has outright control,[59] but the general swing to the left in Britain's unions meant that the Party could often form alliances with other 'left' forces which would often prevail over the moderates. Many of Britain's modern 'left' trade union officials appear to have lost their predecessors' visceral anti-Communism. The General Secretary of the Transport Union, Jack Jones, the President of the Engineers, Hugh Scanlon, and a host of other union leaders have written for the CPGB daily newspaper, *The Morning Star*. The TUC General Council was in the forefront of opening talks with the Moscow-controlled World Federation of Trade Unions, and it invited to Britain, as its official guest, A. N. Shelepin (then a CPSU Politburo member) at the head of a delegation of Soviet 'trade unionists'.[60] In 1977, the TUC General Council refused to condemn Soviet treatment of dissidents even when specifically requested to do so by the Electricians' Union. The TUC, which for most of the post-war period had no CPGB presence on its 25-member General Council, in 1977 had two Communist members on that body. A third, Reg Birch, is a Maoist.

What all of this reveals about the political power of the CPGB must remain open to conflicting interpretations. The tide may be turning against them, following the results of recent AUEW elections. Certainly, it suggests that the CPGB is more of a force in British politics than its miniscule membership and electorate would suggest. In any event, it remains an intriguing case study of CP strategy with regard to organized labour— and, furthermore, in a nation in which organized labour plays a powerful political role within the country, both by acting directly upon the government and by its controlling position in the Labour Party apparatus.

CAUSES OF COMMUNIST STRENGTH

The growth of Communism within societies with something of a liberal democratic tradition is new in the post-Marshall Plan era. For the moment, the reasons for such growth must remain largely speculative. Also, the reasons may differ from nation to nation and may not form a general pattern on a pan-continental basis. Even so, there has been a *general* growth of Communism throughout southern Europe and there may be present, dimly as yet perceived, *general* reasons for it. Similarly, there has certainly been a *general* increase in the acceptability of Communists throughout Western Europe and, likewise, there may be *general* reasons for this. Rather than attempt the hazardous exercise of delineating the precise cause and effect, it may be more rewarding at this stage simply to state the conditions (international, political, ideological, economic and social) which have accompanied the growth (and the growing acceptability) of Communism in Western Europe. There may not necessarily be a connection between them. On the other hand, such an intellectual procedure may indeed help us towards some tentative explanations for the advance of the CPs.

For this purpose, let us take as our two reference points the middle fifties (when the Communist parties were effectively contained, their prospects bleak, and Marxism still a minority intellectual pursuit) and the middle seventies. It was towards the latter part of this period that the West European Communist Parties were seen to come into their own as a serious political force. By 1974, when the Communist-supported candidate for

President of the Republic claimed 49.3% of the vote in France, the PCF grew in confidence and appeared to be pulling out of the doldrums of the Gaullist and post-Gaullist years. The Common Programme, the united left, seemed to be working. By this time the *Compromesso Storico* had already been proposed in Italy and the PCI's powerful showing in the local elections of 1975 made its eventual consummation more likely. By the middle seventies, both a united left government in France and an 'Historic Compromise' in Italy were real and present possibilities. What had changed from two decades earlier?

The changes have been both contextual and intrinsic. During the progress of these two decades, the political context in which Western European Communism has had to operate has changed somewhat. For a start, the fifties and early sixties was a time of considerable East–West (US–Soviet) tension, and of high anti-Communist rhetoric emanating from the highest quarters—usually in response to a similarly vibrant anti-capitalist rhetoric from the Kremlin. The Truman, Eisenhower–Dulles and Kennedy years—the period of the so-called 'cold war'—were replete with direct East–West confrontations (the Berlin crises, the Cuban missile crisis) in which the American international posture was not only anti-Soviet, but also anti-Communist. President Kennedy, in a public speech in 1961, exemplified this posture in words that today would seem to many to be extreme:

> For we are opposed around the world by a monolithic and ruthless conspiracy that relies primarily on covert means for expanding its sphere of influence . . . it is a system which has conscripted vast human and material resources into the building of a tightly knit, highly efficient machine that combines military, diplomatic, intelligence, economic, scientific and political operations.[61]

Kennedy, as did many in his generation, saw international politics as part of a world struggle, as much ideological as anything else:

> 'We dare not fail to see the insidious nature of this new and deeper struggle. We dare not fail to grasp the new concepts, the new tools, the new sense of urgency we will need to combat it—whether in Cuba or in South Vietnam. And we dare not fail to realize that this struggle is taking

place every day, without fanfare, in thousands of villages and markets—day and night—and in classrooms all over the globe.'[62]

That such words today from an American President might appear as discordant simply illustrates the waning of the official high ideological profile of the West since earlier days.

This approach to world politics—seeing it in terms of a struggle against Communism—was prevalent throughout the West before, and for a few years after, Kennedy's Presidency. This view was shared, too, in Western Europe by politicians and leaders of opinion across the political spectrum, and certainly so in the social democratic parties. Gaitskell in Britain, Schumacher and Brandt in West Germany, Mollet and Deferre in France, Saragat in Italy—all would have been at home with this kind of approach and language. In this dominant political atmosphere, in which the global struggle was seen as much as one between 'Communism' and 'Democracy' as between national powers, it would have been extremely difficult for the West European Communist parties, even had they publicly detached themselves from the Soviet Union, to make much headway. The ideological dimension of the East–West conflict (its anti-Communist dimension) was so prominent that the subtle nuances of modern 'Eurocommunism' would have gone both undetected and unbelieved. The Communist parties of Western Europe were ideologically isolated.

Such ideological isolation was complemented by political isolation. Until Mitterrand, the French Socialists (after Socialist Premier Ramadier's expulsion of the Communists from his government in 1947), adopted a policy of total ostracism towards the Communists. In January 1947, the Italian non-Communist left split on the issue of relations with the PCI, dividing into two factions, the Social Democrats and the Socialists. Both factions were prepared, after a while, to enter the numerous centre-left governments without the Communists. After the war, the British Labour Party introduced its proscribed list of Communist front organizations, membership of which was incompatible with membership of the Labour Party. This was abolished in 1973. During the fifties and sixties, the Socialist International refused all contacts with Communists, as did most Social Democratic Parties on an individual basis. So did the democratic trade union movements, both Christian and Socialist. With the decline of anti-Communism, the isolation of the Communist Parties ended.

The decline of anti-Communist rhetoric in the West has coincided with the nominal easing of international tensions between East and West in Europe and the arrival of détente. The effect détente has had upon the acceptability of the Communist parties in Western Europe is difficult to assess. The extent to which détente has been interpreted in the West, though, as a framework for easing the ideological conflict is also the extent to which it has become easier for the European Communist Parties, with their predilection to meld a new found rhetoric of democracy with Communism, to become intellectually respectable.

Another contextual change has been the new power relationship between the United States and the Soviet Union in Europe. The Soviet Union is now the major military power on the European continent. This was not perceived to be the case in the fifties and sixties. With the failure of the Western European nations to evolve the Common Market into more than an economic union and increase their own individual military power, this Soviet preponderance remains a fact of European life.

Allied to this new factor in European politics is the perceived lower resolve of the United States following its defeat in the Vietnam war. American resolve to defend Western Europe may, in fact, be as firm as it has ever been. Indeed, American military commitment is continually being revised, both upwards and downwards; and the European troop withdrawal proposals of some sections of Congressional opinion, so persistent only a few years ago, seem to have waned. Even so, the unquestioning assumption held by most European politicians of the fifties and sixties, with the exception of Charles De Gaulle, about American resolve is no longer intact.

Soviet military power and preponderence in Europe and doubts about American resolve have led some eminent scholars to talk of a 'Finlandization' process at work within the separate European nations.[63] Even if this analogy is overdrawn, changing European perceptions of growing Soviet power and waning, or ambiguous, American resolve cannot encourage an environment which is actively hostile to the European Communist Parties.

Because of these changing power relationships, Western European leaders may feel constrained not to attack major aspects of Communism in Western Europe. For instance, by questioning the loyalty of the Western European Communist Parties to the democratic system, indicating that they cannot be trusted, and that they remain allies of the Soviets, they risk setting in train an anti-Soviet backlash among the peoples of Western Europe which European politicians will not be able to control and which, moreover, will incur the ill will of the Soviet Union. In the absence of countervailing American military power and resolve, this is seen as a very dangerous exercise. This changed perception of big power relationships within Europe may help to explain the nervousness of some of the Western European leaders at the time of President Carter's Human Rights campaign aimed at the Soviet Union.

These contextual developments, either individually or collectively, may help to explain the growth and increasing acceptability of Communism in Western Europe. That they have accompanied its advance may be wholly coincidental. Yet, it seems inconceivable that Communist parties would be near governing in Italy and within distance of power-sharing in France, if the political environment of the fifties and sixties had lasted until today.

The sixties and seventies have witnessed developments other than changes in East–West relations, that may have a bearing upon the rise of 'Eurocommunism'. These changes may be intrinsic to each nation state. Obviously, in Portugal and Spain the presence of officially organized Communism would not be possible at all without the fortuitous collapse of the dictatorships. The Iberian Communists capitalized on the long term investments that they and the Soviets had made in some sections of the underground. As a result, in the immediate post-dictatorship environment, they were able to consolidate their hold over major sections of the trade union movement. As a result of their disciplined organization, they were able to expand quickly to become a significant electoral force. In Italy, where the growth of Communism is particularly pronounced, several factors may be at work. Probably the most important is the declining confidence of the electorate in the Christian Democratic establishment that has ruled the country for thirty years, particularly at a time of rapid social and economic change. Professor Are believes this to be the overriding factor. In France, the PCF has not improved its electoral position for many years; yet it is nearer governmental power today because of its new relationship with the Socialists. If it had not been for the emergence of the united left, then the PCF would remain a large, but contained, phenomenon. In Britain, the CPGB has benefited from the passing away of a generation of social democratic trade union leaders and from the growing acceptability of Marxist analysis; and also from the enhanced power of the trade union movement as a whole.

Much research still needs to be done into the separate national causes (economic and social change primarily) of the growing acceptability of Communism.

Yet, the late sixties and early seventies have witnessed certain pan-European developments (unconnected with the international balance) that, at the very least, have coincided with the growth of Communism. One scholar has written of 'the vague and persistent feeling that democracies have become ungovernable', and that this feeling 'has been growing steadily in Western Europe'.[64] The high inflation and unemployment rates of the seventies; the dislocations caused by the oil price rises; student unrest; the growth of the importance of the media; the decline in social deference and respect for traditional institutions; the increasing size of the education sector and the estrangement of many intellectuals from the system; the growing complexity of government and life itself; the emergence of powerful regional movements; the increased search for equality and the discoveries of new rights; the whole unanchoring process involved in the decline of traditional nationalisms, religion and even class: all of these factors have been advanced to help explain increasing ungovernability. Moreover, it should not be forgotten that the social, economic and cultural changes that it is often claimed are leading to growing ungovernability, are taking place within societies that, for the most part, do not have stable democratic traditions to fall back upon. This is certainly the case throughout the whole of Europe with the exception of Britain and the Low Countries and Scandinavia.

Rapid social, economic and cultural change in a society without a deeply embedded liberal democratic political culture, one that cannot easily assimilate these changes into the democratic process, may itself be a cause of the growth of authoritarian or even totalitarian political forces.

Alternatively, the increasing acceptability of 'Eurocommunism' may have little to do with a growing need for authoritarian political solutions to difficult problems of change; rather, it may simply be the expression of a desire to try new political approaches and leaders. In countries with an historic public resistance to Communism and Communist parties, this anti-regime feeling may take the form of large votes for third parties (like the Liberals or Scottish Nationalists in Britain or the Gilstrup 'anti-taxation' party in Denmark). In Italy, however, anti-Christian Democratic sentiment may channel itself into the PCI, not as an endorsement of its principles or even its programme, but as a protest against the regime. Fading memories of Communist behaviour in Eastern Europe after the war; the short-lived revulsion in the West over the invasions of Hungary and Czechoslovakia; a new generation often ignorant of the past and contemptuous of the cold war—all this, together with a respectable, liberal, 'Eurocommunism' may make support for Communist parties an acceptable and comfortable method of protest.

For the future, another factor that may further enhance the growth of the European parties is the American attitude towards them. Several of the European participants in this study have stressed that American attitudes and foreign policy, whilst not decisive, can be significant. For example, by indicating that American opinion would find the European parties as acceptable partners in Western government, American leaders make the European parties respectable. European Communist leaders appear to be well aware of this; and this may explain why many of them are anxious to visit the United States, even if it means, as in the case of Carrillo, a willingness to cross a picket line of striking workers at Yale University. That European Communist leaders also agree with our contributors about the importance of American opinion to Europeans is further underlined by their sensitivity about American statements critical of their entry into government. The Carter Administration's warnings about Communist participation in the government of Italy (January, 1978) caused considerable consternation in Communist circles both in the Soviet Union and in Western Europe. While it is possible that the Communists are trying to exploit what they regard as a US tactical mistake, such sensitivity may also indicate that American opinion can indeed be an important factor in determining PCI strength.

2 The Communist Parties and Domestic Politics

The term 'Eurocommunism' is now widely used in Western academic, journalistic and political circles. Although official Soviet sources denounce the use of the term as a Western attempt to split the international Communist movement, some western Communist party leaders have recently embraced it as an accurate self-description. Santiago Carrillo enshrines it in the political vocabulary by the very title of his recent book: *'Eurocommunism' and the State*. Other party leaders are more tentative. Berlinguer, for instance, has signalled his acceptance: 'This term was obviously not coined by us, but the very fact that it is circulating so widely shows how profound and widespread the longing is for new kinds of solutions to gain ground and advance in the countries of West Europe . . .'[1] The PCF, the CPGB and several other minor parties also accept the term.

What, then, does 'Eurocommunism' imply? Although it has become a catchword for a description of recent developments within the CPs of Italy, France and Spain, its very usage carries with it some doubtful assumptions. First, it assumes the arrival of a pan-Western European political movement of Communists linked together and united, possessed of a common aim and based upon a unique new political formulation. There is, however, no evidence that a pan-Western European Communism in the full sense, has yet emerged. The leading Communist Parties of Western Europe have few special links with each other which they do not have with other Communist parties in the Eastern bloc. Occasional joint declarations are issued, but no pan-Western European conference has been, or is about to be, called at which the various parties could develop together and codify a unique brand of 'Eurocommunism'. In fact, at the rather unusual gathering of three European parties (the PCE, PCI and PCF) in Madrid in March 1977, the three General secretaries became fearful that their meeting might be interpreted as a 'Eurocommunist' counter-summit to an Eastern bloc gathering in Sophia. The communiqué resisted all but the mildest criticism of the Soviet Union.

Secondly, 'Eurocommunism' is assumed to denote the treading by the CPs of 'national roads' separate from the Soviet path. The national roads policy, however, is as old as the international Communist movement itself. Lenin himself sanctified the tactic of national roads in his pamphlet *'Left Wing' Communism: An Infantile Disorder*;[2] and the CPGB, even in its most Stalinist phase (the early 1950s) under the leadership of Harry Pollitt, was setting forth its case for the 'British Road to Socialism'. The national roads policy within the various parties was well developed long before 'Eurocommunism' was coined. It was a standard feature of an earlier phase of international Communist development.

Thirdly, and more to the point, 'Eurocommunism' is used to describe what is perceived to be a 'new form' of Communism developing in Western Europe. This 'new form' is seen both as sufficiently separate from the Soviet model of socialist development and as having broken free from erstwhile Stalinism. Even more is sometimes claimed for 'Eurocommunism'. It is suggested that the West has little need to fear it, because it is a part of, and will be forced to work inside, the democratic systems of post-war Western Europe; Communist parties in or out of power are locked into the European parliamentary systems.

Indeed, one of the key arguments proffered to support the thesis that 'Eurocommunism' exists at all centres upon the validity of the European Parties' long term commitment to democratic practice and principles. But how deep does this new commitment go? Dr. David Owen, Britain's Labour Foreign Minister, has posed the question:

Is Communism in Europe a latter-day Trojan Horse for

dictatorship and totalitarianism? Or has there been a qualitative change since the 1930s, as a result of which the major West European Communist Parties have a genuine and lasting contribution to make to the further development of a democracy within a framework of individual liberties and pluralist values?[3]

Doubts, obviously, remain. Memories of Communist declarations in favour of democracy in Eastern Europe before the Soviet takeovers there in the late forties die hard. Furthermore, the European parties devalue their new found democratic credentials by continued reference to the democratic systems of Western Europe as 'bourgeois democracies'—systems they remain theoretically committed to replace. Giorgio Napolitano of the PCI offers an intriguing insight into Italian Communist thinking about democracy: 'The objective of the struggle against fascism is neither to establish the dictatorship of the proletariat nor to restore bourgeois democracy purely and simply. It is to create a democratic regime of a new type.'[4]

Western Communist intellectuals still seem to view 'bourgeois democracy' (Parliamentary government, secret ballots, political opposition entrenched in the system) as a transitional system, part of a process towards 'socialism', towards a 'democratic regime of a new type'. Western observers may well wonder what such a 'new' type of democracy will look like in practice.

A further complication is the imprecision of the modern Western debate about the meaning of democracy itself. The old certainties seem to have disappeared. The erstwhile exclusive concentration upon political democracy has given way to wider definitions involving social and economic conceptions of democracy. Human rights are no longer expressed solely in individual and political terms but also in a collective and economic sense. Communist emphasis on collective and economic 'rights' consequently help them to establish a certain democratic legitimacy within the West.

Amid this intellectual and political confusion, how can the question of Communist party commitment to democracy (as we have known it in the West) be resolved? It is difficult to answer this question definitively—unless and until the Communist parties are put to the test of governmental responsibility. A true test would not involve Communists controlling one or two less than strategic ministries; it would, however, involve the Communist party controlling almost all ministries including interior, defense, economic and foreign policy. Yet, if they ever do manage to achieve a monopoly of governmental power it may be too late. Better than waiting for the test of government, some tentative conclusions can already be arrived at by other methods. Are the Communist parties now so reconciled to the democratic process that they have become parties like any other? Do Communist party alliance policies represent an attempt to enter the mainstream of West European politics as part of a permanent reconciliation with other democratic parties—a fusion of organization and ideology? Do the new ideological and policy positions of the Communist parties now no longer place them outside the West European democratic consensus? An attempt will be made to answer these questions in turn.

THE COMMUNIST PARTY AS A POLITICAL PARTY

Is the contemporary West European Communist party different in kind from other political parties in Western Europe? Are the European Communists different in terms of their objectives, their strategy and the nature of their organization?

Unlike the bourgeois parties, the Communists see their aim as revolutionary and irreversible change. They seek to replace capitalism by socialism. They seek to replace the type of political system that has developed with capitalism, most typically described as 'bourgeois democracy', with a radically new kind of system associated with socialism. In short, they seek to transform the fundamental political structures of Western democracy and usher in a new political society.

While European Socialist parties also claim that they seek to replace capitalism by socialism, and sometimes it becomes difficult to disentangle Socialists from Communists, there remain major differences between the European Communists and all other parties, including the Socialists—a point Communists are not loath to proclaim frequently.

When pressed to say what kind of political system they are working towards, the Communists often become vague, taking refuge in obfuscation or in loosely defined future patterns—like

Napolitano's 'democracy of a new type'. Certainly, they claim that their ultimate societies will be both democratic and socialist; yet, they appear to have great difficulty in developing their objectives any further. One indicator, however, of the real meaning behind these concepts of democracy and socialism may lie in the types of existing democratic and socialist regimes that they identify with as models for their own development and those they do not.

While the European parties are frequently at pains to demonstrate that they are building their own type of socialism, they all reject as models the most advanced democratic socialist systems in the world, such as Sweden or Israel. Instead, and significantly, they more readily identify with the Soviet Union and the East European regimes. As Luigi Longo, the President of the PCI, put it recently:

> The Russian revolution has been the greatest work that has ever been done, not just written, and whatever one says, it is a propulsive democratic force not only for the Soviet nation but also with regard to the situation in the world. Can you imagine what the situation in the world would be supposing that this great economic, political, military, yes, also military and ideological force no longer existed.[5]

For years past, the leadership of the European parties has associated socialism with the Soviet Union and its allies. The party press and training programmes have over the years helped to develop a subculture within each of their countries which values Soviet institutions above all others. As will be discussed, each year hundreds of thousands of officials and members from the European parties are lectured on the subject of the superiority of the Soviet system, and they travel to the Soviet Union and Eastern Europe for vacations and education. Judging from the dedicated organization which the Parties put into these trips, and their popularity amongst the membership, the very least that can be said is that the European Parties do not reject the Soviet model of socialist development. Indeed, they value it. And they prefer it to others that are on offer. Similar status is not accorded by the European parties to democratic socialist systems which fall within the Western tradition. Instead, the European Parties castigate democratic socialism.

Although the European Parties have maintained for years that they are independent of the Soviet Union, they rarely criticize the socialist or democratic nature of the Soviet system. If indeed they do envisage any basic differences between their own ultimate conception of democracy and socialism and that operating within the Soviet Union, then they fail to point them out. This is particularly the case with PCF and PCI leaders. Although they frequently proclaim that they no longer intend to model their societies on the Soviet Union and other Communist regimes this simple declaration is rarely accompanied by an explanation about how precisely these 'new' models will be different or, alternatively, what precisely, is wrong with the Soviet model.[6]

Several PCE leaders, most notably Carrillo and Azcarate, have gone somewhat further than their French and Italian comrades. They have suggested that the Soviet Union is not socialist. Yet, they have so far failed to clarify their own particular conception of socialism (except, that is, in the vaguest and most elusive outline) and how it would differ significantly from the Soviet conception.

Perhaps one of the most illuminating indicators of their views can be found in their support for Dubček and his efforts in Czechoslovakia to build 'Socialism with a Human Face'. However, it should be noted that the Dubček regime, while certainly more liberal than its predecessor and more dangerous from the Soviet point of view, was clearly not a democratic regime by Western standards. Dubček at no time indicated that the Czech party wished to move in a social democratic direction and out of the Warsaw Pact. The situation in Hungary, twelve years earlier, was very different. And the Soviet invasion of Hungary was, and is, generally supported by the European parties.

The more advanced and liberal 'Eurocommunists' often assert that the 'transformation to socialism' in Western European nations will occur without the harshness and tyranny of the Soviet experience because the nature of their historical experience is radically different. Yet at no point has any serious writing appeared from these advanced 'Eurocommunists' which sets out in detail how the transformation will actually work.

The simple affirmation of a belief in democracy cannot in itself help to distinguish the European Communist Parties from the Soviet Union, as democracy—loosely defined—has been the professed goal of every Communist party, including the CPSU and the parties of Eastern Europe. While, indeed, the European Parties may be affected by the liberal, pluralistic cultures in which they operate, and this may help to shape their vision, Communist leaders and intellectuals do not explain how this process works. It must remain a bewildering enigma how their recent conversions to the democratic systems within their own societies have not, as yet, led the European Parties away from the Soviet Union as the most acceptable model on offer of socialist development. The European Communist Parties remain distinctly different from all other major European parties in the way in which they continue to identify with the fundamental postulates and practices of the Soviet state.

Furthermore, unlike European Socialists and certainly other European parties, the Communists, in general, still believe that they are the undisputed leaders of the working class. The European Parties see themselves as the decisive leaders of the most decisive class. No one else can fulfill this leadership and directing role; no other class or group of leaders are as important in bringing about the goals of the revolution. No other political party sees itself in this light. These are exclusively Communist notions, based upon an exalted leadership philosophy. The small CPGB argues that it is 'a party capable of giving the *leadership* needed in the struggle to transform the labour movement, strengthen working class unity'.[7] The leader of the larger PCF insists that: 'Building Socialism in France is linked to the capacity of the Communist party to fulfill its *directing* role in the Socialist revolution'.[8]

Again, the PCE differs somewhat from the other European Communist Parties on this question. PCE theory suggests that the classical Leninist formula for the achievement of socialism can now be modified to take advantage of recent societal changes. PCE theorists maintain that now not only the working class but also other 'forces of culture'—the new scientific, technical, administrative, and intellectual layers of the population—can be included in the alignment of forces which will push society towards socialism. This new 'class' theory of revolutionary development for Spain and Western Europe is consciously counterpoised by the PCE to the original Leninist reliance on the alliance encompassing only workers and peasants to achieve the final transformation to socialism. Mujal points out that if the decisive alliance of class is so broadly defined, then the forces interested in the realization of socialism need no longer be conceived as the work of an elite vanguard. Instead, the people, expressing themselves electorally, can gradually legislate socialism into existence without the need to resort to extra-legal means.[9]

Socialists and Social Democrats also seek to bring about major change. They believe that the working class supports their efforts. They draw much of their strength from the support of manual workers and their families, and their politics is often rooted in working-class life. Even so, they are often sceptical about the notion of the working class as an 'historic class', as the agent of revolutionary change. More crucially, they certainly do not see themselves as providing either a vanguard or tribune role for the working class. They are without the political or organizational elitism of their Communist adversaries. Rather, they see themselves as but one of a number of parties competing to represent the interests of workers and other groups in societies.

Another way in which Communist strategy differs from that of other parties is the degree of importance they attach to advancing across a broad front. Parliamentary objectives are important to them, but they also focus upon gaining control of all the major non-governmental institutions of society, what is often described as extra-parliamentary mass struggle. The 'bourgeois' parties, for the most part, concentrate their attention upon gaining control, by electoral means, of the government. Their focus, by comparison, is almost exclusively electoral. They measure their power, for the most part, in parliamentary terms.

Communist Parties seek not only influence in the electoral or governmental arena; they seek to dominate all the important sectors and institutions of society as well. In the statutes of the PCI the party is seen as functioning 'in every aspect of mass political action in the centres of productive, cultural, and associative life which exists in the territory under (their) jurisdiction'.[10] As the CPGB put it: 'The vital need is for an organization of socialists, guided by the principles of scientific socialism, active in all the struggles, in all the unions, in all the progressive movements and able to give leadership to them . . .'[11]

Western European CPs wish to move society, albeit democratically, by persuasion if possible, to a higher form of society from which there will be no return. Democratic parties eschew such chiliasm, accepting instead that their limited objectives will receive setbacks in an on-going structural contest. A member of the Central Committee of the PCI, Lucio Lombardo Radice, has recently been very revealing on this point:

> *Interviewer*: 'But complete individual freedom necessarily implies the legitimacy of a variety of political programmes, including that of saying 'no' to socialism. I'm sorry to harp on this point, but it seems to me crucial.' *Radice*: 'I don't believe any such thing would happen. Would any part of the population want to see a regression from socialism, a retreat from a higher form of society to a lower? Can you see a Hungarian or Romanian agrarian party wanting to return the land to the large landowners?'

About the Italian future, Radice said: 'I'm no prophet; but once the working class has acquired hegemony and led Italian society out of its almost permanent crisis, it would be difficult imagining anyone wanting a regression from a better state of society to a worse state.'[12]

It is this kind of Communist reasoning that leads observers to fear that, protestations about 'multi-party democracy' notwithstanding, even the liberal Communist parties of Italy and France will not easily relinquish power once they have achieved control. To fail to envisage opposition as possible is not far removed from ignoring or repressing it, in the belief that it is unreal or has no value. If change is seen as irreversible, if popular reaction against a higher form of society is excluded as inconceivable, if the hegemony of the working class abolishes class society (and parties are seen as representing classes), *then* the social and political strategy of Western Communist parties would seem to preclude the need for alternative opposition parties under Communism—at least in theory. It appears that the role of the Communist Party is to create a society in which other parties are neither needed nor conceivable.

Communist parties also differ in a major way from 'bourgeois parties' in the primacy they accord to party organization. Indeed, one student of the European Parties has suggested that 'administrative questions about party organization come to have priority over "ideology"'.[13] Communist ideologues sometimes even define their differences with other left parties in an organizational sense. A Secretary of the PCF once remarked that 'the whole history of our party is marked by the resolute struggle against social democrat hangovers in the matter of organization'.[14] Also, the internal organization of the European parties can give some important clues to how Communists would probably organize the wider society when in power. Indeed, Gramsci, the intellectual father of Italian Communism, has gone as far as saying that: 'The party is a model of what the workers state will be tomorrow.'[15]

The organization of all Communist Parties, including the European Parties, is based upon the Leninist model of 'democratic centralism'. In essence, this means that a few leaders of the Party at the top can obtain almost complete control over their members. They have created a machine, a set of institutions, which enables them to determine the broad outlines of Party policy without organized challenges. They select and control the Party's full-time staff and the Party's elected officials. The leaders are also in a position to discipline and expel members. Obedience to the Party line is expected, and usually enforced. This is achieved by a variety of methods; some mechanical and coercive, others educational and cultural. The Democratic Centralist method often involves thorough discussion and persuasion at all levels of the Party. Enormous amounts of time are devoted to explaining the decisions of the party leadership to the members, to self-criticism sessions and to persuading doubting party members of the wisdom of the leadership's tactical and strategic grasp. In practice, democratic centralism proceeds by a dual process of directives and exhaustive persuasion. It aims to ensure order, unity, central direction and discipline. Whilst other parties are to some extent hierarchical, none (save perhaps some of the fringe parties of the extreme right) bear much of a resemblance to the Communists in questions of organizational doctrine and practice.

In every Western European Communist party, as in all CPs, power in practice flows downwards. The statutes of the PCI, for example, are replete with centralized and authoritarian control mechanisms that ensure such uniformity through the organizations.[16] Article 5 establishes the principle of the subordi-

nation of the minority to the majority, of the individual to
the organization, of the lower tiers of the organization to the
upper; a principle guaranteeing absolute unity of action. The
PCI organization system also enables higher bodies to control
lower bodies by a variety of means: in practice Congresses
can only be convened from above; and, to protect the party
from the formation and consolidation of unwelcome 'tendencies'
at the local level, all PCI Directorial Committees and Central
Commissions can meet together to dissolve the Directorial Committee immediately below it (the Central Committee of the
PCI with the Central Control Commission can dissolve the
Regional Committees and so on downwards). Article 5(d) of
the PCI statute of 1964 spells out the same message: 'The
decisions of superior echelons are binding on inferior echelons.'[17]

Power in the Western European CPs is concentrated in the
top echelons of the Party. The structure at the top differs
little from Party to Party. Each Party has a Congress (nominally
the parliament of the party) and a Central Committee (elected
by the Congress). The Central Committee of the PCI has
176 members and, like other Central Committees, is too large
and unwieldy to meet regularly or to take the key decisions.
Usually, in most CPs, the Central Committee elects a Politburo
Executive Committee and Secretariat. The PCI, however, inter-
poses between the Central Committee and the Secretariat a
Directorate of 36 members. The relationship between the Central Committee, the Directorate and the Secretariat (eight
members) is, essentially, that between the parliament of the
party, the government of the party and the cabinet of the
party. Naturally, because the Secretariat can meet several times
a week, it is at all times at the centre of the entire, complex
party machine and has all the various strands of current party
business uninterruptedly in its hands.

The method of selection to these central bodies of CPs is
the core of democratic centralism. As all the subordinate bodies
of the Party are rigidly controlled from the centre, then the
method of constituting the Secretariats and Central Committees
are of great importance. In theory, party officials for each
level are elected by the level directly below it. In fact, each
higher body co-opts from each lower body and the nominating
or co-opting level sends emissaries down to meetings of the
electing level to ensure that the right people are elected. Conse-

quently, the line of authority, the power to designate officials,
flows from top to bottom and the General Secretary, together
with the Secretariat and Politburo, essentially control the bodies
to which they are, theoretically, responsible. Professor Are has
suggested that in the PCI a certain proposition and balance
does exist in the composition of the Central Committee, but
that this reflects general tendencies at the party summit, in
practice within the Secretariat, and corresponds to the Secretariat's view of what it considers useful to represent and to its
opinion on what the picture of the forces guiding the party
should be like.

The PCF's election system is little different. In reality, the
party leadership is determined from above, not below. For
instance, in the election for members of the Central Committee,
the Party Congress which theoretically elects the Central Committee, is presented with a *single* list drawn up by a commission
on candidacy. The Congress can only ratify this list, not add
or elect whomever it wishes. Georges Marchais, at the 1964
Party Congress, justified this procedure as representing the true
spirit of 'proletarian democracy'. He attacked more open
methods of election as 'satisfying the spirit of those . . . attached
to bourgeois democracy with all its formality'.[18]

This method of leadership determination is not conducive
to either the arrival of independent political stars or to the
autonomous representation of political ideas and interests.
Members of the highest councils of the party are co-opted,
not on the basis of their social or political prestige, or for
their independent ability to articulate ideas and interests, but
rather because of qualities most suitable for a party bureaucrat—
perseverance, methodical industriousness and the orderly performance of duties. Consequently, those who get to the very top
of the party machine have an air of dedicated conformity about
them. Years of working within a tightly controlled political
apparatus devalues individual initiative and produces a semi-
permanent nucleus of leaders who run the party. For instance,
Professor Kriegel has pointed out that although there is a heavy
turn-over of membership in the PCF, its leadership remains
remarkably constant. Whilst almost two-thirds of PCF *members*
have been in the party for less than ten years, this is the
case for only 4% of the members of the Central Committee
and the Politburo. More than two thirds of the members of
these governing bodies came into the party before 1958.

The main function of regional, provincial and local bodies is to implement the decisions of the Party summit. Article 13 of the PCI governing statute states in revealing language that the task of regional Directorial Committees is: 'To put the party line into practice in its area and, within this framework, to adopt party policy on a regional level ... It is the main channel by which the summit organizers are linked to the peripheral organizations and govern them.' Consequently, there are no centres of independent local, regional or provincial power within the 'Eurocommunist' party structures. The job of these 'intermediate' levels of organization—intermediate, that is, between local cells or sections and the party summit—is both to forward already-determined policy and to propagandize, raise funds and organize. These intermediate levels of party organization (federations, essentially) often coincide with electoral divisions for the national parliaments and assemblies but, even here, they have little control over the election of CP candidates for office. This is a prerogative of the Central Committee. Most of the democratic parties of Western Europe, no matter how centrally organized, continue to repose the power of selecting candidates for public office in their local constituencies. This power is jealously protected and, unlike the CPs, enables local politicians with a base of their own to emerge onto the national scene.

The basic unit of CP activity traditionally has been the party *cell* which can function at the place of work (usually a factory) or territorially (street or village cells). Lately, though, this particular product of Leninist organizational theory has fallen into disuse in some European parties. Throughout most of Italy, cells exist only on paper; the PCE, even during the Franco era when clandestine operations were imperative, abandoned the cell as compulsory in an attempt to attract new members. The PCF, on the other hand, has been expanding its cells in the workplace rather dramatically; and in the PCP, the cell remains the basis of the whole organization of the party.

In the PCI the cell has been superceded by the *section* as the basic unit of grass roots organization.[19] The PCI section is a much larger organization than the traditional cell; it is organized both territorially and in places of work. At the end of 1976 there were 11,875 sections (for the 1.7 million members) throughout the country. The work of the sections is divided between bureaucratic and administrative duties aimed at internal party consolidation and activities for broadening the party's social and political alliances, such as party propaganda, Communist festivals, picketing, organizing anti-fascist committees and the like. As with the intermediate levels above them, the sections have no autonomous political life of their own. They are organs for transmitting a centrally determined party line. The closely knit conformity in which the sections work sometimes resembles that of a disciplined army and, in organizational terms, presents a favourable comparison to the usual chaos and haphazardness of so much of political life in Italy.

From top to bottom (from the Secretariat down to the section or cell) the CPs of Italy and France are, probably, the single most organized and internally disciplined political forces within their respective nations. Although the adaptation of Leninist organization theory to Western and mass parties has been uneven (particularly with the decline of the cells), its essential features remain; the CP is suffused with an internal authoritarianism that usually enables the party to act as one. It brings to the loosely controlled and pluralistic democratic environment in which the party works a finely controlled political weapon. This puts the Party at an organizational advantage over its opponents.

How is control maintained? One powerful factor, often ignored, is the apparent need that many rank and file party members have for a guided and controlled political environment. They tend to offer little resistance to the authoritarian, paternalistic and centrally directed party machine. Guiseppe Are argues that the PCI's rigid political structure both meets with the approval and coincides with the psychological attitudes and cultural backgrounds of the majority of its members. He suggests that the PCI rank and file does not, in fact, want free discussion because it has a childlike fear of critical debate. It needs simple, categorical truths set out from above. In fact, far from being uneasy with democratic centralism it is proud of the Party's monolithic structure.

To this need for political authority should be added the financial and professional dependency upon the party which cause thousands of party supporters to remain loyal to it. A recent survey has shown that as many as 80% of national and 60% of provincial PCI leaders derive their living from positions occupied by virtue of the party (party, trade union or co-operative officerships). At the electoral level PCI politicians are dependent upon party approval, not upon personal political support based upon individual ability or local interest backing. Consequently, the Party becomes the vehicle for financial support, social prestige and political advancement. This basic dependency is also a source of strength for non-Communist parties in democratic countries; yet, when basic dependency upon a party machine is linked to a structure of democratic centralism, dependency upon the party means dependency upon its central leadership. The CP professional political activist cannot bargain as between party factions, a traditional source of political independence in other parties.

The most dependable and loyal group of all within CPs are the permanent officials. They are the life-blood and nervous system of Communist party organization. Exact figures for the number of permanent officials in CPs in Western Europe are difficult to assess. The parties tend to obfuscate on this subject. According to Cunhal's report to the PCP Central Committee's Eighth Congress, however, the Portuguese party has 507 full-time officials. Probably, permanent officials on the direct payroll of the party number in the low thousands for both the PCI and the PCF. But on top of these official 'apparatchiks' must be added the thousands of party 'militants' who work full- or part-time in all the municipal, business and trade union organizations the party controls.

A further source of control for Communist leaderships over their rank and file is the pervasive disciplinary apparatus of the party. Typical infractions of discipline include attempts to mobilize 'minority' opinion by exchange of information and circulation of separate documents; attempts to form 'horizontal' links between party organs (horizontal links between party organs at the same level usually are forbidden); contacts, exchanges and meetings held outside the statutory bodies of the party; attempts to convene congresses without the approval of an immediately higher body; general disloyalty involving a challenge to the democratic centralist system itself, or refusing to be bound by the majority line. Discipline is enforced by a hierarchy of punishments which lead, ultimately, to the expulsion of a member.

PCF leaders, for example, receive detailed information about their members from open and secret channels through which

actual or potential infractions of the rules are reported to them.[20]
There is no proof that the PCI has secret control mechanisms,
but permanent control over the political activities of all individual members, control over the grass roots of the party, is
guaranteed by the very structure of the PCI itself. All the
PCI Directorial Committees (at section, provincial, federation,
regional and central levels) have Party Control Commissions
established alongside them. The task of these Commissions is
to examine disciplinary questions and to co-operate with the
Directorial Committees in ideological instruction and in the
development and use of party cadres. The Control Commissions
are the recipients of many private accusations by party members
against other party members. Members, who are accused of
breaches of discipline, are tried in true democratic centralist
fashion, (and their continuing membership is determined by
bodies immediately superior to those in which they hold membership). For instance, a provincial Directorial Committee,
liaising with the provincial Control Commission, can expel
a member of any section in the province.[21]

Party control over Communist legislators is an important
and little known fact of Communist life. Apart from Marxist-
Leninist theory about the dominance of the party machine
over parliamentary groups, which all Communists adhere to,
such a subjugation of parliamentarians to the party is guaranteed
by the dependency of the elected politician upon the party
for his or her survival. Most European electors vote for the
Party and not the man; hence, party approval is a prerequisite
for electoral success. This is also the case in non-Communist
parties in the West; but in these parties factionalism within
the party allows its legislators some area for maneuver. For
instance, the British Labour Party employs an open—rather
than a democratic centralist—party organizational system and,
in consequence, a majority of the Parliamentary Labour Party
effectively opposes the left-wing majority within the party
organization. Of the 73 PCI Members of Parliament who sit
on their party's central bodies (the Central Committee and
the Central Control Commission), as many as 65 were themselves
PCI permanent officials before they became Members of Parliament. Not only is their seat in parliament dependent upon
the party machine but so is their prospective livelihood if they
should lose elected office. Communist parties often prefer to

derive their legislators from among their permanent officials: this guarantees loyalty and obedience and further cements the parliamentary group to the party machine.

A parliamentarian's loyalty to his party is an important factor in a successful political career in most political parties in Western Europe. An essential difference between the non-Communist parties and the CP's is the lack, in the CPs, of *local* loyalties. Many Western parties, where there is an electoral system of constituencies (as opposed to party lists), leave the selection of candidates to local constituency branches (sometimes with a national approval mechanism, which is usually a formality). CP candidates for national office (Senators, Deputies) are selected instead by national organizations. For instance, PCI candidates for Parliament are, essentially, selected by the Central Committee of the party. In reality, therefore, PCI and PCF Members of Parliament are responsible not simply to the 'party' (as opposed to the wider electorate) but to the party leadership. It is of no little significance that the party-induced turnover rate for PCI deputies and senators is higher than that for their equivalents in the Christian Democratic Party.[22]

Indoctrination and training of party cadres play an enormously important role in consolidating the leadership's control over the party. This takes the form of both informal day-to-day discussions in the cells and sections and formal training programmes. Democratic parties, too, have political education and training programmes for their members. Even so, the education within these parties is altogether less systematic and rigid. For instance, the leadership does not always control the party educational programmes or organizations; the philosophical teaching is eclectic; account has to be taken of party factions; and training is often little more than an attempt to help party members project themselves to the public at election times. The aim is to make the membership more informed, articulate and persuasive in its dealings with the public—not to create a disciplined, centrally controlled cadre system.

Communist parties, on the other hand, are characterized by an enormous amount of discussion and analysis. This is to ensure that the leadership's views are accepted by the membership. At all levels of the party an inordinate amount of time and energy is spent by party functionaries in persuading party members of the wisdom of the leadership's position.

Appeals are made to the membership to support every twist and turn of the leadership's position on the grounds that the leadership of the party is in the best position to understand the forces at work at any historical juncture. Appeals are also made to the membership to keep the party united in the face of the splitting activities of the bourgeoisie. Hence, every active member is subject to constant monitoring and attention from his section or cell leader. Each individual member is subject to a barrage of party propaganda from both the party press and local party comrades. This ensures that all but the most recalcitrant individuals are brought into the leadership's fold.[23]

Sometimes, as Machete maintains in the case of the PCP, the European parties call upon the Soviet Union for the 'education' and training of their members. The PCF and PCI, however, have resources to provide their cadres and new recruits with their own training programmes. Both parties provide a great number of part-time and residential courses for the party faithful. The PCF provides an eight-month residential course for party members at its central school in Paris, as well as a host of other less rigorous courses held throughout the country. The PCI has expanded its political education quite dramatically since 1972, when it possessed only one central school of Communist studies. Since then, six new party schools have been set up (four inter-regional ones, one inter-provincial and one provincial) covering North, Central and Southern Italy. Professor Are estimates that between 1972 and the end of 1974, 14,885 people passed through these party schools, having taken courses of varying length. The PCI also offers courses at the local level, and it has estimated that as many as 130,000 'students' have passed through this system since 1970. An interesting feature of CP educational policy is that it is aimed at all levels of party organization reaching up to members of the Central Committee, who attend the party's central schools (usually unaccompanied by 'lower' officials). The PCI, at local sectional courses and seminars, has recently attempted to attract non-party members who, together with local militants, can engage in open discussion.

For party members, the content of this 'political' education has three aims: to enable their personnel to organize and direct specific political campaigns (for instance, the referendum on divorce held in Italy in 1974); to provide technical training about elections, party organization and the like; to ensure ideological consistency throughout the Party and adherence to the Party line. Although the Southern European CPs (particularly the PCI) have attracted some notable scholars and intellectuals of late, the supervision of lectures and seminars is still very much in the hands of internal party ideologists and organizers. This helps to guarantee doctrinal orthodoxy and strict adherence to the momentary tactics of the party.

In sum, 'Eurocommunist' CPs, unlike traditional non-Communist parties, seek a systematic and radical change in the political, economic, social and cultural environment in which they operate. To bring this about, the vanguard parties must be able to manoeuvre in a pluralistic, capitalist environment and yet remain true to their revolutionary aspirations. This needs sophisticated political tuning, exercised from the top of the party, and carried out faithfully throughout its entire structure. Hence, the continued adherence to Leninist democratic centralism. In matters of party organization little compromise is allowed; for the most part, the rigid and centrally directed inner-life of the Western Communist parties continues to describe an essential, qualitative, difference between them and the democratic parties of the West.

Although all political parties retain features of organization which are hierarchical, the democratic parties of Western Europe are usually 'open' or 'pluralist' in nature (reflecting the kind of society within which they operate and wish to retain). For instance, democratic parties allow for the operation of open factions. Such organized factions can bid for wider support within the party, often using the media as a means of appeal.

In the Leninist parties the formation of factions is extremely difficult. When they do appear, however, the party, through expulsions or resignations can usually avoid prolonged intra-party political warfare.

Indeed, even dissenters who attempt to win over their comrades on specific issues, are usually not tolerated. The parties argue that they need the entire party to support their policies, and that they cannot afford the luxury of factions. Hence, the rights and ability of the minority to become the majority, the hallmark of the democratic process, are not to be found in Communist parties.

The French and Portuguese Parties appear to be the least

tolerant, and the Spanish and British the most. The Italians are somewhere in the middle. In general, though, once the parties' top policymaking bodies reach their decision and explain it to the membership, dissent is supposed to, and usually does, cease. Those who do not cease dissenting are usually disciplined and, if necessary, expelled.

In France, the expulsion of Roger Garaudy from the Politburo and Pierre Daix from the Central Committee were just the latest in the PCF's long history of excommunicating its own leaders. In Portugal, the most prominent expulsion of recent years was that of Martins Rodrigues, a member of the Executive Committee in 1964. In Italy, the Manifesto group, a liberal faction, was expelled in 1969, and leaders critical of the Soviet Union, such as Galluzzi, have been removed from sensitive posts.

In Spain, the party has been more tolerant of open differences in the leadership. At the 1968 Central Committee vote to ratify the Executive Committee's condemnation of the Soviet invasion of Czechoslovakia, there were five dissenters. After that time, various Stalinist dissident factions, the most famous of which was led by Executive Committee member Enrique Lister, were tolerated, and then left the party. More recently, Mujal points out that there have been votes in the Central Committee in which a number of people abstained or voted against the Executive Committee. At the 1978 PCE Party Congress a significantly large minority voted against the leadership on key issues. Unanimity is no longer always the case. The British Communist Party, too, tolerated a Stalinist faction for some time. This group, led by Sid French, left the party in 1977.

An interesting historical point is that there is no example of a Communist party leadership which has been overthrown by an opposing faction without support from Moscow.

Democratic parties, on the other hand, allow open discussion at all levels of the organization, and divided votes are a commonplace. Such debates are often heated, and the results of ballots are sometimes unpredictable. In the Communist parties, the top leadership decides upon the party position on each issue in advance. At meetings of the party, these decisions are endorsed, almost always unanimously, by the delegates. It is not without irony that when the PCF decided to drop the 'dictatorship of the proletariat' as an official party goal, this decision (which broke with a fundamental postulate enshrined in party tradition) was approved without a single dissenting vote at the Party Congress.

In democratic parties, officials and leaders are usually elected by some kind of genuinely democratic process which often involves the grass roots of the party. In parliamentary systems it is often the case that the parliamentary leader, sometimes also the party leader, is elected by the parliamentary caucus only. But the Members of Parliament, who make up the caucus, are often subject to genuine challenges within their constituency parties by party members of differing political persuasions. In Communist parties, officials at all levels are selected solely by the party leadership. Also, democratic parties do not subject their members, who work in non-party organizations, to the strict discipline exerted by Communist parties. CP members in other organizations receive detailed instructions from the party leadership as to the policy stances they should take within their organizations. Failure to obey these instructions can often result in expulsion from the party. It is instructive to counterpoise the control which, for instance, the PCI or the PCF exercises over its members in their respective national trade union movements with the freedom of British Labour Party and West German SPD members. It is regularly the case that, acting in their trade union capacities, members of the non-Communist parties will contradict and attack the official policies of their party leaders. There are very few Communists who follow this pattern.

THE COMMUNIST PARTIES AND THEIR ALLIANCES

Even though the European Communist parties remain different from other political parties—particularly, in terms of their ultimate political goals and their internal organization—they have rarely been loath to form alliances. The Communist party in Western society shuns isolation. Alliances for intermediate goals with other parties and between 'the working class' and 'progressive, non-proletarian' forces have been an intermittent feature of Communist activity since the days of Lenin. Western Communists have long since abandoned the view that the European parties can, in all circumstances, do without the aid of bourgeois parties. The Communists see no prospect of coming to power by Soviet-style putsch, or in the Eastern European style with support from the Red Army. They also doubt they can form governments alone, by collecting a majority of the votes in free elections. The parliamentary road to socialism whether it be Italian, French, British, Spanish, or Portuguese, is, of necessity, to be paved with alliances, as several way stations are passed before the socialist transformation can be achieved.

The European parties have, historically, sought to create three different kinds of alliances according to the needs of the prevailing situation. A 'United Front' includes the Communist party and other left parties, such as Socialists (and involves an attempt to unite the whole proletariat). A 'Popular Front' includes, but goes beyond, the left and embraces progressive middle-class groups and parties as well. A 'National Front' (formed when nations are attacked other than from the Soviet Union) includes all patriotic elements, even sections of the military. These alliances, in practice, can take the form of formal electoral agreements (or pacts) with other parties (such as operated in France after 1972); co-operation with other parties for specific political objectives (as in Britain during the Common Market referendum campaign of 1975 or in Italy during the divorce referendum of 1974); support or abstention in parliament to sustain non-Communist administrations (as in Italy from 1976); and Communist participation in and support for coalition governments in a number of European countries after the Second World War.

The attempts on the part of Communist parties to join with other parties in alliances is sometimes interpreted as a willingness on the Communists' part to make the democratic, 'neo-capitalist' system work. Alternatively, it is argued that irrespective of their aims, the current alliances of the parties are locking them in to a democratic system which they cannot change or break loose from, even if they wished. As one American democratic socialist has put it: 'It is a question whether mass (Communist) parties, increasingly integrated into the social life of their countries, *can* be revolutionary.'[24] Hence, the European parties, so it is assumed, have a stake and an interest in the existing system—rather like other parties. From this assumption flows the argument that Communist participation in government will be a stabilizing force in the long as well as the short run. Finally, it is assumed that a continued and expanded association with democratic society and other political parties (the apparent erosion of the 'state within a state' of 'society within a society') will affect the democratic centralist organization of the parties and contribute to their genuine democratic evolution.

Certainly, the mass Communist parties have at times contributed to the stability of democracy. In Italy, the PCI, since the emergence of the campaign for the *compromesso storico*, has studiously avoided giving the impression of seeking to polarize Italian society. It has co-operated in combating and condemning terrorism and in reducing inflation. Also, the PCE has helped to avoid polarizing Spanish society in the post-Franco era.

Yet, although Communist parties may, in certain circumstances, have an interest in defending and stabilizing the democratic system, this (by the admission of their own theorists and leaders) is only a staging post *en route* to their ultimate destination.

They must at all costs avoid a right-wing backlash. Giorgio Napolitano has put the point this way:

> If the workers' movement confines itself to a mere denunciation of the contradictions of the capitalist system and of the responsibilities of the old ruling classes and carries out actions purely in defense of the interests of the workers, then it locks itself into a rather restricted and unmaneuverable position. It isolates itself and gives fuel on the political level to that right-wing maneuver: the *reactionary* counter-offensive we were speaking of a moment ago.[25]

Hence, democracy must be secured against reaction, but only as a prelude to the long-term aim of the radical transformation of society towards socialism and communism. Alliance policies are forged and broken in order to meet this requirement. Hence, alliances with other parties are not seen as long term mechanisms which will allow the Communist parties to take their full part in the democratic process; rather, they are marriages of convenience, subject to divorce and reunion, often at a moment's notice.

Of course, other parties use alliances in a cavalier manner, as a means to achieve their own political ends. Yet the alliance policies of democratic parties are of a wholly different character. They are part of a process of manoeuvering, with the aim of gaining power within the democratic state. They are not seen as temporary arrangements in order to further the transformation of the state into a wholly different political system. Democratic parties have a stake in the democratic system, because it is the very system which gives them their life and meaning, and allows them to function. Like the National Socialist Party in Weimar Germany, Communist Parties have a stake in the democratic system only insofar as it is part of an evolution towards a radically different political system—in their case 'socialism'.

Socialism used to be identified by the European parties with the interests of the Soviet state. Hence, in the thirties and forties, Communist alliance policies were determined in Moscow. Anti-fascist Popular Fronts were set up in France, Italy, and other countries in 1934; but when Moscow switched direction in 1939, the European parties supported the Nazi-Soviet pact and the Popular Fronts were abruptly ruptured. After the German invasion of Russia in 1941, the Parties reversed themselves yet again and joined National Fronts. After the war, both the PCF and the PCI entered into government as junior partners until they were excluded in 1947, when the Soviets again switched direction. Under Soviet influence, the two parties then embarked upon an opposition phase, with the PCF and PCI even attempting to sabotage the post-war economic recovery of Europe and strongly opposing the Marshall Plan. The PCI, goaded on by Moscow, reverted to a policy of confrontation, but without the vehemence of the PCF.

Italy

The experience of Fascism in Italy was an important factor in the PCI's less sectarian approach, in its attempt to keep some form of alliance policy alive. Indeed, in the environment of fascism or authoritarianism, or in their aftermath, Communist parties tend to forge wide alliances in order to secure the democratic base in which they can freely operate.

During his imprisonment in the late twenties, Gramsci reflected upon the strategic mistakes of the Left which he believed had contributed to the perversion of socialism and to Mussolini's ultimate victory. He came to the conclusion that the central problem was sectarianism, manifested within the Left by the schismatic tendencies of each leftist party, including the Communists. Sectarianism also affected the Left's relationship with the larger society, for the leftist parties and their urban worker supporters were isolated from the masses of the peasantry and from the majority of the intellectuals. Gramsci's analysis of this period is now widely accepted by PCI intellectuals and strategists: 'Gradually the road was mapped out to avoid new defeats in the future and, above all, to defeat fascism by achieving the vastest possible *front* for the struggle against it.'[26] In short, *broad* alliances are necessary to preserve democracy against fascism.

In this sense, alliance policy must be constructed so as to secure the democratic revolution first, so that the socialist revolution may follow without a reversion to reaction. Democracy is a stage towards socialism. It is not an end. It is a means.

It is out of this need for *breadth* in alliance policy that the PCI strategy of the Historic Compromise has emerged. The *compromesso storico* exists on two levels. First, it is conceived in *social* terms as an attempted temporary unification of a broad range of diverse social groups, including both the proletariat and what the PCI terms as 'the Catholic masses'. PCI leaders seem so anxious to allay the fears of the Catholic masses that they have toned down both their anti-clericalism (much more so than the Socialists) and their economic collectivism.[27] Secondly, it is *political*: the attempt to secure a party alliance in government between the PCI and the Christian Democrats.

This *social* content in the Historic Compromise is an attractive and seductive propaganda point with the bourgeois politicians. The aim of bringing together potentially conflicting groups in order to stabilize the system—with the PCI implicitly promising to control proletarian revolutionary ardour in its 'red' regions and in the trade unions—appeals to a national longing for order. PCI leaders realize that such an appeal to order, unity and authority (the proclaimed aim of the *compromesso storico*) is a vote winner. Although the PCI has increased its vote in almost every national election since 1946, it has only broken through the 30% barrier since its 'Historic Compromise' matured into official PCI policy.

The *broad* alliance policy of the Italian party, with its aim of reassuring the potentially hostile groups and classes, was reinforced by the events in Chile in 1973. The failure of the

Allende experiment is regularly referred to by PCI spokesmen as the bitter fruit of too narrow a front policy, which polarized the society and allowed the forces of reaction to counter-attack. Consequently, the *compromesso storico* will not lightly be abandoned as the central medium-term strategic objective of the PCI. It remains the most ambitious, indeed daring, strategy for power of any Communist party in the West.

Spain

The Iberian Communist parties, emerging from years of exile and clandestinity, also face the problem of potential reversions to right-wing authoritarianism. Indeed, both the Spanish and Portuguese democracies are, arguably, even more fragile than the Italian variety. The PCE, particularly since Carrillo assumed the leadership in the late 1950s, has demonstrated formidable flexibility and skill in what, for it, has always been a largely hostile environment. Even as early as 1956, and at Carrillo's instigation, the party issued a call for National Reconciliation. It welcomed the participation of democratic Catholics and even Falangists in an effort to overthrow Francoism peacefully, a process at that time it believed would only take a few years, Since then, the party has been pulled by two conflicting forces: one, urging the party to steer clear of involvement with Francoist institutions (or the Francoist successors in the new institutions of the post-Franco era); the other arguing for some *modus vivendi* between the PCE and Franco's heirs, an accommodation which is considered a prerequisite for the consolidation of democracy and for the PCE to play an important role in Spanish politics. Carrillo has sought to steer a middle course between these positions.

For the moment, the PCE appears to see its primary immediate objective as working with the Spanish Premier and the King to ensure the consolidation of the democratic institutions of the country. This is obviously very much in its own self-interest as the PCE is still small and has decided to take advantage of the democratic environment in order to expand. Yet, its alliance policy is both subtle and flexible. On the one hand, it is already working with the forces of the Centre-Right. Carrillo frequently meets Prime Minister Suarez. It would appear that this type of alliance adds considerably to the respectability of the PCE. From the Centre-Right's point of view, the growing respectability of the Communists limits the appeal of the Socialists. Yet, on the other hand, the PCE has proposed an alliance with the democratic left in the past, and it appears to keep open the option of an alliance with the Spanish Socialists (PSOE) for the future.

As Mujal suggests, it may only be a matter of time before the two parties of the left work out a Common Programme on the French model. The PSOE is eclectic, possessing several different currents of opinion. Some of its leaders claim to be revolutionary and Marxist. For its part, the PSOE does not in principle object to the notion of United Fronts. Even so, the PSOE, for the moment, looks upon the PCE with suspicion. Felipe Gonzalez, General Secretary of the PSOE, has criticized Carrillo and the PCE because, while Communists claim to be working for a democratic society, they do not practice democracy within their own parties.[28] In Gonzalez's view, this makes the Communists unreliable allies for the democratic socialists.

If the PCE's short term strategy remains one that seeks to stabilize democracy in Spain, and this is the burden of Carrillo's writings, then it may alternatively eschew a United Front with the Socialists for fear that this might polarize Spanish society too precipitously. Even so, its relatively poor showing in the 1977 national elections may mean that it will be forced back into a united left strategy, because it has no other option. The Socialists and the Communists achieved together over 36% of the vote in 1977.

Portugal

The PCP, although operating in a fragile post-authoritarian political environment, seems less determined than its Iberian neighbour to ensure the success of democracy as a staging-post to the socialist transformation. After the overthrow of Caetano in 1974, the PCP attempted to secure complete control of the government and even organized a thinly disguised putsch in 1975. In some respects the PCP leadership, particularly Cunhal, appeared to believe that the Portuguese situation was similar to that operating in Russia in 1917. Portugal is less developed than most West European nations; unlike Italy, and arguably even Spain, the consolidation of democracy in Portugal as a stage on the socialist road is unsuited to what is potentially a Third World revolutionary situation.

Although the PCP attempted a quick seizure of power in the early years of the new Portuguese democracy, and seems unconcerned with enhancing the democratic phase, it is not an isolationist party. The history of PCP alliance policy suggests that there is no connection between its unreconstructed Stalinism and a narrow conception of alliances. Its alliance posture retains a flexibility not matched by its ideological rigidity. Indeed, it refuses to make ideological concessions as part of its search for alliances. Its tradition of collaboration with non-Communist groups and parties was forged during the Salazar–Caetano years. The party was banned during this period but arranged, during the heavily supervised elections: 'to work within the other opposition groups—democrats, liberals, republicans, and socialists—whom they sought to draw into a common front'.[29] Furthermore, in the aftermath of the overthrow of Caetano, the PCP reached beyond civilian alliances and into collaboration with and support for the Armed Forces Movement (MFA), which ran the country in the period leading up to the election of 1976. Cunhal himself served in the provisional coalition government which was established by the MFA; and following the formation of the Socialist party's minority government (which excluded, amongst others, the PCP), the PCP continued to argue that the Party should be allowed to take its place in the Cabinet.

The future direction of PCP alliance policy remains unclear. The PCP is not prepared to dilute its hardline ideology and its pro-Moscow orientation in its search for allies, and this has harmed it with the Socialists. The PCP leadership seems content, for the moment, to consolidate its control of the trade unions and the strategically important Alentejo region near Lisbon and, more generally, is seeking to take advantage of disaffection among the peasants and the urban working class caused by the continuing crisis in the Portuguese economic system.

France

Unlike its Iberian and Italian neighbours, the PCF operates within a relatively stable, democratic system, and it has few memories of domestic fascism. Unlike the PCI, it seeks no Historic Compromise and had seemed content with a 'left unity' approach. The 1972 Common Programme, with the Socialists, was reminiscent of the Popular Front of the thirties although, intriguingly, it was not termed as such. The aim of its left unity alliance policy was not, evidently, to assuage the fears of its political opponents on the right and unify the nation (as in Italy), but rather to advance itself into government in coalition with the Socialists. Yet, in September of 1977, it sought a pretext for abandoning the Common Programme.

Almost all non-Communist observers believe that the PCF had made a clear-cut decision not to maintain the alliance with the Socialists even before the negotiations between the two parties collapsed. One account maintains that the sequence of events was as follows: the Left Radicals walked out of discussions aimed at updating the pact, because they were unable to agree to PCF nationalization demands. The PCF then rejected Mitterrand's compromise proposals as not even worthy as a basis for discussion. It has been suggested that the PCF leadership rejected Mitterrand's compromise proposals of the evening of 22 September without proper time to study them in full, and that *L'Humanité* on the following day, carried an attack upon Mitterrand that went into print before the Socialists had made their final concessions.[30]

The reason for this abrupt reversal of alliance strategy remains unclear. It is possible that the PCF misjudged the political effect of the Common Programme, in that in the period leading up to the 1978 elections, it appeared that the Socialists were emerging as the major party of the left, the position which had been occupied by the PCF for most of the post-war period. Also, it is possible that the role of junior membership within a coalition government of the left might not be enough of a reward for the responsibility the PCF might have to take for the continuing economic problems of the country.

In any event, the abandonment of the Common Programme on the eve of the 1978 elections serves to illustrate the unsettled nature of PCF alliance policy. Evidently, its five year march to a 'Eurocommunist' position involving the abandonment overnight of 'the dictatorship of the proletariat' and its declaration in 1973 that it was willing to work with all 'proletarian and democratic forces' and with 'forces representative of the popular masses of Catholicism'—is not contingent upon an unbreakable alliance with the Socialists. It would seem that its immediate political objective is to keep its historic position as the major party of the French left. In such a position it obviously hopes that it can become the main repository for those disaffected with the government.

Yet, the PCF remains stuck on an electoral plateau of about 20% support from the French voters. Without an alliance with the Socialists, it would appear that, in the medium term, it will find it difficult to enter government. This, however, may not be its immediate aim. The PCF shows every sign of believing that the French economic crisis will deepen, and it does not appear willing to take responsibility for it, whilst remaining a junior partner in government to the Socialists. Evidently, PCF alliance policy is not in favour of helping to stabilize French democracy and the economic system when it is not in its own interest. This is not the kind of strategy which would be followed by a party that is fully integrated (locked in) to the democratic system with an interest in making it work.

United Kingdom

By comparison with the mass parties of Southern Europe, the small parties of the North have far less room to manoeuvre in alliance strategy, as they have much less to offer. The CPGB has, for many years, seen its main route to power and influence not through an open alliance[31] with another party, but rather through increased influence within the trade union movement and, through that, within the Labour Party. In this sense, the CPGB's alliance policy is effectively a policy of penetration. The British party makes no attempt to hide its immediate strategic objective: 'The arenas of struggle between the left and right trends include the trade unions . . . and the Labour Party . . . changing the politics of the Labour Party is bound up with changing the politics of the working class.'[32] Furthermore, the precise mechanism for future CP alliance with the Labour Party was spelt out at their 1977 Congress: 'Communists want to restore to the trade unions the democratic right to elect from among those who pay the political levy, delegates of their own choice from those who pay the political levy to the Labour party.'[33] At the moment, although CP members on trade union governing bodies can help determine the way their trade union delegation votes at Labour Party conferences, only Labour Party members can attend these conferences. The aim of the CPGB is to get the Labour Party to abandon this role so that members of the Communist Party can attend policy making (and executive-forming) conferences of the Labour Party under the guise of trade union delegates. Hence, an indirect affiliation of the CPGB to the Labour Party, which avoids the public odium (for Labour) of a direct and formally declared link. There is some support for this strategic objective from within the left-wing of the Labour Party,[34] although it is unlikely to be achieved this side of a general election. Leading figures within the Labour Left appear to want to improve contacts between the British Labour Party and 'Eurocommunist' parties on the European continent. No doubt as part of this rapprochment Labour's left-wing-controlled National Executive Committee invited many of the Western European Communist parties to send observers to its Annual Conference at Brighton in October, 1977. This was a radical new departure for the Labour Party. The CPGB's firm support for the PCI and PCF may help it internally—in its domestic relations with the Labour Party—in the future.

The British situation reflects an acute dilemma for Communist alliance policy in countries where the CP is small electorally, but where it has been able to gain a foothold within the trade unions. The CPGB has no prospect of developing a mass political base, nor of electing enough, if any, Members of Parliament to hold the balance in the House of Commons. Yet, it continues to proclaim its objective of 'alliance, not isolation'.

The long-term, though often forlorn, hope of the small Communist parties in countries where there are large entrenched Social Democratic parties lies in the slow process of affecting the internal development of these parties. As far as the CPGB is concerned, its hope must be that Labour will transmogrify into a fully fledged Marxist party. Alternatively, or complementarily, the CPGB will work on the industrial level to change society.

The past history of the alliance policies of Communist parties, both mass and small, does not demonstrate a desire on their

part for permanent integration into the democratic process. Socialists and Social Democrats, most typically the objects of Communist alliance strategy, have often believed that overtures from the Communists for the formation of United or Popular Fronts presaged on the Communists' part a willingness to work for a genuine and lasting reconciliation between Marxism, or indeed Marxism-Leninism, and democratic values. Yet Socialists have often suffered as a result of this naive optimism. The alliance strategy of Lenin and the Bolshevik Party, the behaviour of the PCE (including Carrillo himself) towards the non-Communist republicans in the Spanish Civil War and the role of the Communist parties in Eastern Europe after the Second World War (their betrayal and infiltration of non-Communist left parties)—all have contributed to a continuing suspicion among the left about Communist Party motives. Aneurin Bevan, the unofficial leader of Labour's left-wing in the 1950s, summed up this feeling over twenty-five years ago: 'The Communist does not look upon the Socialist in common cause. He looks upon him as a dupe, a temporary convenience, as something to be thrust aside ruthlessly when he has served his purpose.'[35]

It is not at all clear that much has changed as far as the aims of Communist alliance policy are concerned since Bevan issued that warning. Alliance policies may no longer be determined in Moscow, but they still possess many of the characteristics of the alliance policies of the thirties and forties.

First, alliances so far do not appear to have affected the internal development of the Communist parties. The European Communist parties are careful to ensure that alliances in no way compromise their own character and goals. Whatever changes may be occurring within the parties are the result of autonomous developments, not an 'infection' by the other parties to the alliance. For example, the alliance policy of the PCP in no way dilutes its Stalinist ideology. Also, alliances with other parties (whether in the form of the Common Programme or the sought-after Historic Compromise) have not, with the exception of the PCE, weakened the tight internal discipline of the Communist parties. Indeed, party discipline which ensures a united body of cadres becomes essential for Communist party political activity in the West. Without such controls over the inner life of the party, the leadership would have less freedom of action to engage in tactical alliances which are subject to overnight changes. Shifts in CP alliance policy can often cause dissension within the ranks of the party.

Second, no European party, not even the very small ones with little electoral future, perceive alliances as preludes to the disbanding of the Communist party apparatus and its fusion into another working class party. Such a development is unthinkable. No matter how small the party, how apparently secure an alliance, how profound the revision of ideology, the Communist party is to remain a permanent feature of each national situation. It retains what it describes as its special role which it believes it alone is uniquely fitted to play. This special role, involving the notion of a higher understanding of historical development, can only mean that Communist parties have little to learn from alliances. Nor do they see the need to adapt and change, except tactically, because of them.

Third, the European parties' alliance policies continue to display a picture of rapid and unpredictable shifts. This, too, is reminiscent of the thirties and forties, even though they may not be at the behest of Moscow. The rupturing of the Common Programme in France, after five years of an apparently maturing and stable relationship between the PCF and the PS, is a recent example. Even the *compromesso storico*, the apparently settled and determined aim of the PCI, has not been inviolate. Recently, the still powerful PCI leader, Luigi Longo, pointed out to the Party faithful that the historic compromise was not to be construed as a permanent arrangement. It was merely a tactical alliance that the party believed was useful at this time. Lenin, he pointed out, also believed in this type of tactical alliance. Indeed, in January of 1978, the PCI, in the wake of the fall of the Andreotti government, threatened to reverse its whole strategy and attempt to form a left coalition government, which would exclude the Christian Democrats from power for the first time in 35 years. The fact that these abrupt changes are no longer determined by a directing centre from outside the country does not make the Communists any more reliable as allies than in the past. In fact, there is little reason to believe that the Communists are locked in to the democratic system. Although some non-Communist, and perhaps even some Communist, analysts may believe that the parties' objective interests are centered in their alliance with bourgeois parties and their support for the bourgeois system, the Communist leaders themselves have not come to this conclusion. Alliances, and ostensible support for stability, are useful tools for the parties. When in their view they become obstacles, they can and will be discarded—even if this does not appear to the bourgeoisie to be in the Communists' interests.

Although Communist alliance policies remain as unpredictable as ever, and show little evidence of a long-term reconciliation with the democratic system, many Europeans today seem less sceptical than in Bevan's time about forging alliances with them. Although suspicion remains, recent CP ideological and policy changes—the whole phenomenon described as 'Eurocommunism'—has allayed some of the fears.

POLICY, IDEOLOGY AND THE DEMOCRATIC CONSENSUS

Do recent ideological and policy changes within the European parties imply the emergence of a new form of Communism that no longer threatens democracy and pluralism? Are the European parties, irrespective of their continued Leninist organization, now a part of the post-war West European democratic consensus? Or, if they are not yet a part of it, do they no longer threaten it? Have they become a branch of Social Democracy?

To describe this democratic consensus by giving it a title is difficult. 'Neo-capitalist democracy' or even 'social democracy' are increasingly used; 'democratic pluralism' in its political, social and economic manifestations would, perhaps, be accepted as providing the lowest common denominator of agreement for the variegated political traditions and parties that make up the Western European consensus. The key ingredients, which make up this democratic consensus, are: respect for the traditional, liberal, political, civil and religious freedoms; multi-party democratic procedures; the preservation of a mixed economy (between public and private enterprises); the autonomy of voluntary organizations (particularly trade unions). Every major Western European non-Communist party or school of political thought would unambiguously accept these four propositions and would fall within the consensus they describe. Some West European political forces would give greater emphasis to some than to others (and there would be a keen

debate over the proportions of the mix in the mixed economy—
although all would be accepted. Most observers would accept
that the neo-fascist National Front in Britain, the MSI in Italy
and portions of the Popular Alliance in Spain would be outside
this democratic consensus. The question remains: are the principal Communist parties also outside it? It is against each of
the four propositions which describe this consensus that the
'Eurocommunist' parties can be measured.

In attempting such a measurement, it becomes clear that
the European Communist parties are ambiguous about their
commitment to these democratic precepts. Also, there is almost
no analysis about how these democratic postulates will function
(and be safeguarded) in their ultimate Communist society.
Furthermore, the behaviour of the Parties in practice frequently
remains disquieting.

European Communism and Political Freedom

The most precise statement about freedom issued by the West
European Communist parties came in the form of a joint declaration by Marchais and Berlinguer, following bi-party talks
on November 17, 1975:

> All those liberties which are the fruit of the great democratic
> bourgeois revolutions or of the power struggles of this century,
> which had the working class at their head, must be guaranteed
> and developed; and thus, the liberty of thought and expres-
> sion, of the press, of meeting and association, the right to
> demonstrate, the inviolability of private life, or religious liber-
> ties, the total freedom of expression of currents of thought,
> and of every philosophical, cultural and artistic opinion.

The PCE's Eighth Congress (held in Bucharest in 1972)
also produced a list of freedoms that it would respect and
at the same time renounced any attempt to impose an official
state philosophy. The CPGB also proclaims its support for the
standard list, but its litany has a qualification: political and
civil freedoms are to be respected 'subject only to those limi-
tations required in any ordered and just society to protect
citizens from interference and exploitation by others and to
safeguard democracy'.[36]

Although 'Eurocommunist' ideologues see an historical connection between the growth of political freedoms and the bourgeois revolutions of the 18th and 19th centuries, they draw
few conclusions from this kind of statement. They would hotly
dispute Jean-Francois Revel's point that there is a continuing
relationship between capitalism and freedom. Revel suggests
that political democracy 'clings to its (capitalism's) back' and
that 'no other form of economy has borne democracy'.[37] Yet,
rarely, if ever, do 'Eurocommunists' address the question
whether political freedoms are *necessarily* accompanied by a
plurality of economic interests and types of ownership. Rather,
because of this lack of analysis, they tend to assume that political
freedoms will be ensured irrespective of social and economic
arrangements—as though politicians can simply proclaim them,
and they will consequently exist.

This lack of analysis of the origins of political freedom differs
radically from the liberal tradition. And it is a precarious intellectual foundation for the continuance of freedom within a
'Eurocommunist' society. If governing politicians within a 'Eurocommunist' society change their minds about the desirability
of freedoms, it is not clear upon what social-economic pillars
the reality of freedom can rest. Also, 'Eurocommunists' retreat
from the liberal tradition of freedom by emphasizing its collective
as opposed to its individual nature, and by setting freedom
in economic and social terms more frequently than in political
terms. For instance Napolitano, in describing his democracy
'of a new type', talks of the need to give it 'an advanced
economic and social intent',[38] but he does not spell out what
he meant by this. For the 'Eurocommunist' freedom (social,
economic *and* political) is magically extended by the transformation into socialism. The exact process whereby freedom is
enhanced, and a description of what such freedom looks like,
is rarely spelt out.

'Eurocommunist' declarations about freedoms must also be
compared to 'Eurocommunist' practice. The culture of Western
European CPs hardly encourages free discussion or initiatives
from below among the cadres who would presumably run an
'Eurocommunist' state. The constant habit of all CP leaders
of rewriting their own history is also a bad omen;[39] as is the
ideological hegemony they attempt to establish in all the cultural
and intellectual organizations that they control (publishing

houses, daily and weekly newspapers, university faculties and other centres of opinion). Also, the PCI, in particular, has a recent history of attempted censorship. Among other activities, it has made proposals for the outlawing of certain foreign television broadcasts that are hostile to the PCI.[40] Berlinguer and his associates also supported a Soviet attempt to persuade the Andreotti government to cancel a *Biennale* Arts Festival in Venice, which was to feature a discussion of 'cultural dissidents in Eastern Europe'.[41] PCI-controlled committees of printers and journalists, as they gain influence over newspaper editors and publishers, ensure favorable editorial and news treatment for the PCI.[42]

'Eurocommunism' and the Multi-Party Democratic Process

Communist parties in Western democracies have long given up Leninist violence as a necessary means of achieving their political aims. Khrushchev's Twentieth Party Congress speech in 1956 put the Soviet seal of approval upon 'the peaceful road to socialism' for CPs operating in highly developed capitalist countries. 'Peaceful', however, need not necessarily mean 'parliamentary' or 'constitutional', for most West European Communist Parties still adhere to the strategy of extra-parliamentary mass struggle; they increasingly declare themselves as bound at this historical juncture by constitutional democratic processes:

> The French and Italian Communists favour the plurality of political parties, the right of opposition parties to exist and act, the free formation of majorities and minorities and the possibility of their alternating democratically, the lay character and democratic functioning of the state, and the independence of the judiciary.[43]

For the French party particularly, this was something of a reversal; only five years previously Georges Marchais had declared:

> We do not believe that the struggle for socialism should be inspired by the system of alternative government that, as

in England, allows the Conservatives and the Socialists to take turns in power to inflict the worst possible injuries on the workers.[44]

The PCE, the CPGB, and most other West European CPs (apart from the PCP) are now squarely committed, 'declaratively' at least, both to the democratic road to power and the maintenance of a pluralist political system in the immediate aftermath of their electoral success.

Yet, fears remain. One reason is that the Communist conception of pluralism is significantly different from that of Western tradition. Liberal pluralism has a spontaneous character about it, assuming that new ideas and political groupings may emerge at any moment from any point in society. The Communist concept of plurality is not spontaneous, but controlled. All kinds of associations can indeed exist and can even be created and directed by non-Communists; but they have no real social or ethical legitimacy, if they do not contribute towards the supreme aims of the society laid down by the directing power (the party). Are compares this view of pluralism to that of the medieval Church, which not only accepted, but often encouraged, the proliferation of a large variety of bodies, but only on the condition that each of them accepted the place, character and function which the Church ascribed to it. Each of them should recognize that the Church alone had the right to define society's prime aims and basic norms of behaviour. As with the Medieval Church, so with a governing Communist party, 'Eurocommunist' or otherwise. It is difficult to imagine a powerful 'bourgeois opposition' being able to function properly in this kind of society.

Other political parties and forces may be *legally* safeguarded under 'Eurocommunist' society, but the conditions may not exist in which they can operate properly. According to their own generally accepted CP class analysis, the socialist societies to which they are moving will remove the vestiges of class society and with it the bourgeois political parties which represent the exploiting classes. The CPGB, in a revealing pronouncement, has suggested that under Communist rule:

The Tory Party's position would be further weakened by the measures taken against its principal backers, the big monopolists, and by the steps taken to break monopoly control of the press, and to open up the mass media to the working people . . .' and, more ominously, 'by the measures taken by the government to tackle the crisis in the interests of the people.[45]

Consequently, there is no need to alarm liberal democrats by pronouncing the outlawing of other parties, if the very process of social transformation will do the job more effectively. 'There can be an objective basis for the existence of different parties in the period of *construction* of socialism',[46] but after the *achievement* of socialism CP ideologists become vague. All rights will be guaranteed, certainly, but what about the reality? In Napolitano's 'democracy of a new type' it, according to Radice, 'becomes entirely unhistorical as well as unreasonable to suppose that they (the electorate) would want to turn the clock back'.[47]

The fragility of a multi-party system under 'Eurocommunist' rule would be further underlined by the polarized and tense political atmosphere in which CP leaders would be likely to enter the government. None of the Latin nations in which the CP is near to power (or power-sharing) has a history of stable democratic development; and an extreme right reaction to Communist participation in government cannot be ruled out. PCI and PCE literature is replete with 'coup' and 'counter-coup' scenarios born of a clandestine and conspiratorial mentality forged in the years of fascism and dictatorship. The PCF too has lived through volcanic political circumstances, both during the Second World War and in 1958 and 1968. Yet, ironically, it is Carrillo who has been the most specific in keeping the 'Eurocommunist' door open for a return to revolutionary means: 'if the dominating classes close the democratic paths'.[48] He has argued that, in the event of a Communist victory: 'There may be a subversive reaction from a section of society . . . if there is an attempt by force from reactionary quarters, then one has to respond with force'.[49] The CPGB puts it this way: 'If parties hostile to Socialism turned to the use of force . . . to sabotage the democratic process, the Socialist government and the working people would use whatever force was necessary to defend democracy'.[50] This type of strategy for resisting undemocratic challenges to a democratic state might seem unexceptionable. Yet when they are enunciated by those who use terms such as reactionary and democracy so loosely, a pause for reflection is in order.

Furthermore all the 'Eurocommunist' Parties supported the use of force (including Soviet troops) to put down the uprising in Hungary in 1956, though not in Czechoslovakia in 1968. The distinction between the two invasions that is drawn in Communist literature is intriguing. In Budapest, according to PCE executive committee member, Manuel Azcarate, 'the enemies of socialism . . . were trying to take advantage of existing liberties';[51] this was not the case in Prague. Radice suggests that to talk of 'counter-revolution in Czechoslovakia in 1968 is pitiful nonsense. In Prague, no one even remembered the names of the former factory proprietors and landowners'.[52] What if they *had* remembered their names? Moreover, what if they wanted capitalism restored? 'Eurocommunists' tend to draw a distinction between legitimate (i.e., 'Socialist') protest against Communist regimes and counter-revolutions. How 'Eurocommunist' governments would define the essential features of a counter-revolution is the key test of their newly acquired democratic credentials. Would a strike be considered counter-revolutionary?; would mass protests (of an obviously non-Socialist character) be tolerated? Future Communist governments in Italy and France, should they come into power, would probably have to operate in this environment. Their continuing refusal to believe that a popular base will exist for turning the clock back, once they are in power, may lead them to mistake democratic opposition for 'clerical fascist' reaction. Indeed, in a real sense, those who wish to return to pre-Communist society will indeed be counter-revolutionaries, and they may be treated as such.

'Eurocommunism' and the Mixed Economy

Each CP, taking into account its national situation, takes a differing position on economic policy. There is a major divergence, for example, between the approach of the PCI and that of the PCF. The PCI has for the time being abandoned its erstwhile commitment to extend the public sector 'which today is big enough'.[53] It intends, instead, to meet its immediate objectives by a vaguely defined National Plan which would set targets for public and private enterprises alike. This very limited approach may have something to do with the general posture of the PCI as a party seeking 'a government of national salvation', willing to make sacrifices of dogma in order to help deal with the crisis. Alternatively, it may be the result of PCI appreciation of the discredited and corrupt reputation of much of Italy's public sector and part of their policy to present an image of the honest party. At the same time, the PCI proposes massive increases in social expenditure which, in Italy's present acute financial situation, will inevitably heighten inflation and 'weaken the power of the bourgeoisie'. The PCI proposes price controls if inflation gets out of hand—with consequent bankruptcies in the private sector.

It would seem that the PCI's overriding strategic aim is to achieve power as a responsible and national party—and to that end it appears to be willing for the moment to sacrifice virtually all of its socialist economic objectives.

The same is not true for the PCF. The French Party originally agreed (in 1972) to a Common Programme with the Socialists which included the 'nationalization of the banking and financial sector of the economy, including insurance, nationalization of armaments, nuclear, pharmaceutical, aeronautical and space industries'[54] and 'government control' over a wide area of other industries. The nationalization proposals of 1972, though significant, allowed Mitterrand to claim that his agreement with the Communists had preserved a 'diversified, multiple, extremely extensive' private sector (the official profits of all the companies proposed for nationalization were only $250 million in 1976).[55] The Common Programme floundered on the insistence of the PCF that a vast increase in nationalization should be agreed. Evidently, the political situation had changed significantly since 1972 when the PCF was willing to agree to a limited programme.

The two major Communist parties of Western Europe seem to view their economic policy (particularly nationalization proposals) as a lever in the power game, to be pulled back and forth according to prevailing circumstances and strategic thinking. The PCI restrains itself on public ownership at a period when it is near power and wants to appear respectable and national; the PCF uses the nationalization issue to break up the Common Programme (which it wants to do, for separate political reasons). In each case, the needs of political strategy supercede the integrity of economic platforms.

The PCE, emerging as it is from a clandestine past and concerned, for the moment, to ensure its place in a fragile democracy gives a low priority to nationalization. It has no carefully worked out economic policy, although it subscribes in the long-run to the principle of extensive nationalization.

Whatever the disparities between each CP's immediate economic objectives, the fact remains that their ultimate collective aim—indeed, the very reason for their being—is the replacement of capitalism by socialism. To Communists the world over the replacement of capitalism means the eradication of private capital accumulation; under socialism the means of production (and possibly exchange and distribution, too) will be under public ownership. This ultimate Communist goal, adhered to by all the 'Eurocommunist' parties, is incompatible with the continuance of the mixed economies of Western Europe. It is, perhaps, a feature of our uncertain intellectual environment in the West (and of simple, wishful thinking) that this point is so often missed as we focus upon immediate policy proposals.

Of course, during the transition to socialism, we can expect the coexistence of public and private forms of property and production. No Communist party suggests that this transition will be swift. Carrillo suggests that during the stage of transition there will be a recognition of the 'role that is represented by the private enterprise'.[56] This recognition, though, is only transitional.

'Eurocommunism' and the Autonomy of Voluntary Organizations

In an industrial society, the degree of freedom accorded to voluntary organizations and, particularly, to trade unions is a valuable test of freedom in society generally. The ability of voluntary associations of workers to bargain and campaign can often be a guide to general societal attitudes toward other, less powerful, autonomous organizations. The Communist parties of Western Europe all claim to respect the autonomy of organized labour; indeed, they have been in the forefront of campaigns to defend free trade unionism under dictatorial and fascist regimes.

Yet, a question remains about their motives. Classical Marxist-Leninist theory has it that trade union militancy within a capitalist society is a means of increasing class consciousness and advancing towards socialism; trade unions, as we understand them in the West, are no longer necessary when socialism has arrived. The Communist-controlled trade unions of Western Europe seek to transform society, not reform it; hence, according to Marxist-Leninist theory, to put themselves out of business.

The attitude of the European Parties to trade union militancy since the Second World War has been uneven. There is no general pattern which would suggest a permanent desire on the part of the CPs for militancy on all occasions. Indeed, the PCF played a major role in holding back a general strike during the tense days of 1968. And the PCI, as it nears power, uses what influence it has with the unions to restrict their demands. Even so, if either party were to go into outright confrontation with the government, then they would encourage trade union militancy. Trade unions, in other words, are seen as an arm of political action; indeed, as a mechanism for creating a society in which genuine trade unions will no longer be necessary.

'Eurocommunist' parties, significantly, have rarely criticized the Soviet Union and the Eastern bloc regimes for their suppression of workers' rights and trade unionism. In fact, Soviet and Eastern bloc 'trade unions' have established a network of relations with Communist (and other) unions in Western Europe. Although there are some differences between Moscow and some of their West European trade union comrades, they work together through bilateral programs and the Soviet-controlled World Federation of Trade Unions to promote the Soviet concept of 'trade unionism' in the Third World.

HAS 'EUROCOMMUNISM' BECOME 'SOCIAL DEMOCRACY'?

On the face of it, 'Eurocommunism' (in the form of *proclamations* about respect for political freedoms, the democratic process, the mixed economy and the autonomy of voluntary organizations) cannot be clearly distinguished from traditional West

European Social Democracy. And the increase of official contacts between Communist Parties and Social Democratic parties in Western Europe[57] may herald some form of ideological 'convergence'.

Yet, it is the Communist leaders themselves who resolutely deny any such convergence with social democracy. Even Santiago Carrillo, the most 'adventurous' and 'liberal' of 'Eurocommunist' theorists, sets his face like flint against any such suggestions: 'Before being a Social Democrat, I would be a Maoist, Trotskyist, terrorist.'[58] Similar, though less dramatic, disavowals of convergence with social democracy issue forth from each Western European CP.[59]

The adamant drawing of such a determined theoretical distinction, on the part of the Western European CPs, is intriguing. Notwithstanding an apparent convergence about the need for pluralism and liberties, social democracy is perceived as 'a sort of bourgeois political thinking. It administers very loyally to bourgeois society and does not intend to transform it.'[60] Few modern 'Eurocommunist' ideologists would dispute the classical denunciation of social democracy contained, and updated, in the 1961 Party programme of the CPSU: 'The right-wing of Social Democracy has completely broken with Marxism and contraposed so-called democratic socialism to scientific socialism. Its adherents deny the existence of antagonistic classes and the class struggle in bourgeois society . . .'[61]

The heart of the dispute centers around the Eurocommunist acceptance, and the social democratic rejection, of the governing precepts of Marxism-Leninism; and of the central role which Marxism-Leninism assigns to class analysis and struggle. Few modern social democrats accept either the classical or the neo-Marxist analysis of the role of the working class in capitalist or neo-capitalist society. While fully aware of the adversary relationship between man and labour at the bargaining table, they do not see the reality of class conflict in the Marxist sense. The British social democratic tradition, Europe's most intellectually powerful, has insisted upon the objective of class harmony.

'Eurocommunists,' on the other hand, adhere, in all its essentials, to the classical Marxist-Leninist position on class. Even so, 'Eurocommunist' class doctrine has undergone a softening process. The 'dictatorship of the proletariat' is no longer used by most Western European Communist Parties, including the PCP. The 'Eurocommunist' parties now adhere to Gramsci's formulation of the 'hegemony of the working class.' How exactly this new formulation differs from 'the dictatorship of the proletariat' remains obscure. Neither 'dictatorship' nor 'hegemony' in regard to state power has ever been properly defined either in classical or in modern Marxist texts. 'Eurocommunist' theologians simply assert their commitment to the process of 'working class hegemony' over the society rather than assign any new meaning to it except to explain that the older formulation may have created an image of repression in untutored minds. Neil McInnes suggests that the suppression of the 'dictatorship of the proletariat' 'means something and can have tangible effects' and that 'the abandonment of the doctrine would acquire its full significance only if it were presented as a juridical innovation'.[62] No such systematic linkage of the doctrine of hegemony to a new non-Marxist bourgeois judicial process has been attempted by any of the 'Eurocommunist' parties. Hegemony serves not to describe a new revolutionary process; rather, to create a more favourable image in bourgeois eyes. Even so, for liberals, 'hegemony' is still a fearsome term. It does not sit well alongside pluralism.

Another aspect of the 'softening' process of 'Eurocommunist' rhetoric towards class is a refinement of working class alliance analysis. Today's West European CP statements are replete with appeals beyond the 'working class' towards new classes that are seen as having an interest in the transformation of society. These new classes are, typically, described as 'intermediate strata' (intermediate, that is, between the working class and the capitalist class). They include: middle-grade management within the State apparatus, self-employed professionals like architects, lawyers, writers, artists, doctors and family businessmen and women who employ no workers.[63] CP strategists see this 'intermediate strata' as becoming increasingly disaffected as the crisis of capitalism develops, and the possibility emerges of winning them over to radical, even socialist, ideas and action. Yet, it is important to realize that this new CP interest in (and courting of) new middle classes, supplements rather than replaces older theories, leaving the fundamentals of the old class analysis intact. The 'working class' remains the primary agent of socialist change; there is no fusion of classes into a new revolutionary class; the 'intermediate strata' are *allies* in the struggle for socialist transformation, not the leaders of it; there is no reassessment of the belief in the class nature of society. The alliance between the 'working class' and the 'intermediate strata' is simply an updating of the older, Leninist, notion of the necessary alliance between the proletariat and the peasants or the rural semi-proletariat.[64] As Italian, French, Spanish and other West European societies continue to develop, industrialize, bureaucratize, and 'embourgeoisify', the CPs see no need to alter or abandon their class analysis; rather, they simply graft onto the classical analysis a modernized 'petty-bourgeois' appendage. Lenin, probably, would have approved.

Consequently, the supplanting of 'dictatorship' by 'hegemony' and the arrival of an 'intermediate strata' in no way abridges the fundamental Marxist-Leninist class analysis which underpins the philosophy of the European Parties. Put simply, the essence of this analysis (accepted by all the West European CPs) is that capitalism is a stage of historical development characterized by class struggle; that the working class, aided by its class *allies* and led by the Communist party, will establish Socialism by one means or another; that the socialist society, thus created, will be classless and the epoch of bourgeois culture, economic organization and political institutions will be over.

This is the key point at which the acceptance of the class doctrines of Marxism-Leninism collides with the 'Eurocommunist' claims of liberty, pluralism and democracy. For, if bourgeois society is to be transformed into socialist society, are all the bourgeois freedoms and political procedures to be transformed as well? Are the great bourgeois-democratic advances of the 18th, 19th and 20th centuries (advances which Communists recognize) carried over into the 'Socialist' state? *Or*, are they simply carried on *for a period* during the 'construction of socialism?'. Alternatively, are they abandoned during the construction of socialism only to reemerge in some undefined, magically-enriched way in the nirvana? Professor Leszek Kolakowski, the Polish Marxist philosopher (now living in the West), has grappled with these questions. He has argued that:

No matter how Signor Berlinguer explains that representative democracy is a 'strategic' and not a 'tactical' principle . . .

this could mean that democratic rules could be valid for a longer, not a shorter, time under Communist rule; or it could mean that they will last until the next 'historical stage' which is inevitably bound to come when the moment is ripe.[65]

The assumption here is that *at some point* the 'democratic rules' (the product of the bourgeois revolutions) no longer remain valid under socialism.

The problem for the 'Eurocommunists' is that the 'democratic rules' they claim to support are couched in static terms, whereas the philosophy to which they adhere is dynamic, articulating a process of revolution (or evolution) which may or may not carry along with it the bourgeois freedoms so important to non-Communists. While 'Eurocommunists' continue to straddle both horses, the debate about freedom within a 'Eurocommunist' society can never be resolved.

There is little evidence, however, that the 'Eurocommunist' parties with, once again, the possible exception of the Spanish, are evolving to the point of a break with their Marxist-Leninist past. Their policy shifts are not supplemented by a radical re-thinking of the fundamental precepts of Marxism-Leninism. It is of little relevance simply to denounce Stalinism. It is Marxism-Leninism that separates Communists of all kinds from Social Democrats, Christian Socialists and even large sections of the democratic socialist tradition. Some factions within the Socialist parties adhere to a Marxist (indeed a Marxist-Leninist) analysis. The French, Italian and Iberian Socialist parties include both Marxists and non-Marxists in their ranks. In Northern Europe, the British Labour Party's left-wing has historically owed more to Christian Socialism than to Marxism. In West Germany, the SPD formally overthrew Marxism as its official ideology at the Bad Godesberg Conference of 1959.

Are the European Communist parties now in a position to make, in the words of David Owen's question, a 'genuine and lasting contribution' to the democratic system as we have known it in the West? Certainly, the European parties have moved nearer to the democratic consensus. They are now ambiguous about the role of the working class and their own vanguard role in society. One of the parties, the PCE, has become somewhat more tolerant of dissent within its own ranks. Through their alliance policies, some of the parties have demonstrated at least a short-term commitment to the stability of the democratic system. Also, significant aspects of their doctrine have undergone radical declaratory changes.

Yet, amidst all this change and movement, the European parties still remain committed to revolutionary goals and (with the exception of the PCE) still basically take the Soviet Union as their model for development. They still retain for themselves a special position as a party unique from others; and they still aim at irreversible systemic change. The parties still adhere to democratic centralism and ensure a high degree of uniformity amongst their members. Their alliance policies are not stable, and are still subject to rapid changes; and they admit that they are tactical. As far as doctrine is concerned, their whole intellectual structure remains, at bottom, Marxist-Leninist, and where changes have taken place, the way in which these developments fit in to their overriding intellectual framework is confusing. They still are unable to present an alternative philosophical system that is coherent and convincing.

Under these circumstances, it is difficult to conclude that the parties in their present form are now in a position to make that 'genuine and lasting contribution' to democracy.

3 The Communist Parties and the International Balance

One of the crucial developments of recent years within the international Communist movement is the growth of obvious public tension between the Soviet Union and alternately the PCE, PCI, PCF, the CPGB, as well as several other small parties. This apparent developing polycentrism is one of the main pillars on which the edifice of 'Eurocommunism' has been built. It has given rise to the view that the European parties are basically independent of the Soviet Union and that their increased strength or entry into government could even be a net liability for the Soviet bloc.

However, the nature and degree of the tensions between the European parties and the Soviet Union are unclear. The debate between Moscow and the principal European parties is complex, suffused with subtleties, ambiguities and contradictions. Moreover, an analysis of the perspectives of the European parties on important subjects such as participation in Western defense, European co-operation or the development and alignment of the Third World does not lead to the conclusion that the parties have become a net liability for the Soviet Union. Indeed, while there may be disadvantages accruing to the Soviet Union from the increased strength and independence of the European parties, they remain, whether in or out of power, useful in Soviet efforts to shift the global balance against the West.

THE COMMUNIST PARTIES AND THE SOVIET UNION

Although there are differences on a number of questions, the nub of the dispute between Moscow and the European parties appears to centre around the need, as Moscow sees it, for strict observance of 'proletarian internationalism'. This is the accepted term in the international Communist movement for putting Soviet interests first, and for recognizing Moscow as the sole centre of Communist authority. As the CPs of Western Europe—led by the Italian and Spanish—have developed their separate notions of national roads to Socialism, and as a conscious effort has been made to distance themselves from certain aspects of Soviet existence, then the Soviet insistence upon 'proletarian internationalism' has been increasingly challenged.

This challenge culminated at the All-European Conference of Communist Parties held in Berlin in June, 1976, and attended by all the significant European CPs. A communiqué was issued following the conference that was ostentatious in its omission of any reference to the principle of 'proletarian internationalism'. Although not specifically rejecting the notion, the communiqué, instead, referred to 'the mutual solidarity among working peoples of all countries'. It insisted upon the independence of each Communist Party and upon non-interference in the internal affairs of any one by another.

The PCF was in the forefront of the battle to reject 'proletarian internationalism'. For some time previous to the Berlin Conference, Marchais had been criticizing 'proletarian internationalism' as serving the interests of Soviet state policy over that of the national revolutionary needs of French Communism. At the various preparatory meetings prior to the Berlin Conference, however, it became clear that none of the major CPs would attend if 'proletarian internationalism' were to be on the agenda.

The fact that the principle of independence was so clearly established at Berlin gave some theoretical legitimacy to those criticisms by various CPs of the Soviet suppression of human rights. All the major West European CPs claim to be democratic and to believe in free expression. They consequently deplore certain selected aspects of both of the Stalinist past and the Soviet present.

The European Parties' support for Soviet dissidents has

received wide publicity, but this support has been selective. On the whole, the CPs of Western Europe speak up in support of the '*Socialist* Opposition' in the Soviet Union and Eastern Europe. For instance, through their Party presses, they give extensive coverage to Roy Medvedev,[1] the Communist dissident, and to the Charter 77 group with Czechoslovakia. Some of the European parties criticize the invasion by the Warsaw Pact of Czechoslovakia in 1968, because they believe the Dubček regime was essentially socialist. No support, and little coverage, is given to other types of dissidents: those Soviet Jews who wish to emigrate, the Solzhenitsyns and Bukovskys, the Sakharov faction, or to those concerned with workers' and trade union rights. In short the Western European Communist parties' protestations of their own democratic and human rights credentials are more thorough-going and all-embracing than is the support they render to those trying to promote democracy and pluralism in the Soviet Union and Eastern Europe. Even so, as Professor Schapiro points out, the support for dissidents, limited and selective though it may be, could become a major problem for the Soviets.

Moreover, until recently, no Communist party in Western Europe had followed up its criticism of the lack of human rights in the Soviet Union with a systematic analysis of the political causes of such suppression. No link is made by the European parties between Communism and denial of liberties. Indeed, Santiago Carrillo has suggested that Soviet society is not 'Socialist' (by which he means Communist) and that consequently this, to him, explains many of its imperfections. The other Communist Parties proclaim that the Soviet Union, while essentially a 'socialist nation', possesses certain elements of 'degeneracy'. Hence, neither Carrillo nor the leaders of other CPs can bring themselves to consider the point that a systematic cause and effect exists between the Communist character of the political and economic system in the Soviet Union and the suppression of intellectual, ethnic, and worker dissidents.

The European parties' occasional criticisms of the lack of freedoms in the Soviet Union must be set against their *generalized* support for Moscow—a political empathy between the Communists of Western Europe and the Soviet Union which clearly does not exist between those same parties and the United States or any other western nation. This *generalized* support is typified by Giorgio Napolitano, a member of the eight-man PCI Secretariat and its spokesman on economics: 'We cannot ignore the ideological bonds and the feelings of solidarity with the Socialist world (Communist world—Soviet Union and Eastern bloc) . . . Nor can we accept that the international role of the Soviet Union in the struggle against imperialism and for peace be ignored or denied.'[2]

With the possible exception of Carrillo and some of the Spanish Communists, the CPs of Western Europe believe the Soviet Union to be a 'Socialist state', and, consequently, it is more like the society they are seeking to achieve than the societies—the capitalist societies—that they at present inhabit. In other words, the Soviet Union, despite some errors, has moved to a higher level of social organization than Western societies. This pro-Sovietism, at the most basic level, is a crucial distinction between the European parties and all the democratic parties of Western Europe. The Soviet Union is also viewed, as expressed in the Napolitano quote, as 'peaceful'. An assumption is made by the West European Communists that it is the United States, not the Soviet Union, that is 'aggressive'.

The anti-imperialist rhetoric of the European parties also operates to the USSR's advantage. Here again, the Western European CPs, including the Spanish, side with the Soviet Union against the West. The assumption is omnipresent that imperialism is a Western capitalist phneomenon. At no time has any Western European CP described Soviet control of Eastern Europe as 'imperialist'. Carrillo has said that: 'The United States gives itself the right not only to use violence against the oppressed classes of its own country, but to exploit whole peoples, just as every colonial empire has done recently.'[3] No such reprimand is administered to the Soviet Union. Oppression, exploitation, violence are all, evidently, exclusive products of the Western system.

Not only do the Western European CPs (with the ambiguous exception of Carrillo) believe the Soviet Union, for all its imperfections, to be 'socialist', 'peaceful', and 'anti-imperialist' but all resist and oppose a phenomenon they describe as 'anti-Sovietism'. Anti-Sovietism is a term appended to wholesale denunciations of the Soviet system—which the European CPs never make. In fact the communiqué issued after the Berlin Conference specifically rejected anti-Sovietism. There is no rejection by the European Communist parties of 'anti-Americanism'.

This natural, ideological preference for the Soviet Union is not affected by the human rights issue. Although selectively critical of Moscow's behaviour, the European Parties do not allow their limited espousal of human rights to draw them into the Western camp. On this issue most favourable to the West, the European Communists take a neutral stand between East and West. They denounce both sides, criticizing the West for the denial of human rights caused by endemic unemployment and discrimination against women and other 'minorities'. These social and economic rights are given as high a priority as political rights.

The generalized support for the Soviet Union (as a socialist society, a force for peace, and as anti-imperialist) may explain why the West European Communists support Soviet foreign and defense policy. Indeed, with some important, though ambiguous, exceptions in Europe (such as European integration and membership of NATO, the French deterrent and American bases in Europe), the European parties generally find themselves in harmony with Soviet global policy; and they frequently work together to promote the destruction of Western imperialism in Europe and throughout the rest of the world. As PCI President Longo put it in praising Leninism and the Soviet Union: 'Can you imagine what the situation in the world would be, supposing that this great economic, political and military, yes also military and ideological force no longer existed.'[4]

THE COMMUNIST PARTIES AND EUROPE

The major foreign policy focus of most European parties is, of course, Europe. They are nothing if not ambitious about the impact they hope to have on political evolution throughout Europe. Some, such as Carrillo, see in Europe a future model for international Communism. As the Spanish leader put it: 'Whether one likes it or not . . . the Socialism in Western Europe will become a pole of reference for the whole working class movement.'[5]

In its present form, however, Europe is too 'capitalist,' and too dependent on the US. The aim of those European CPs that are interested in European integration is to work through the European Communities (EC) to effect change, both in the internal political and economic systems of Western Europe and in Europe's international outlook.

Involvement in the EC is seen as part of a more general European-wide strategy. The major CPs work at various levels within Europe, not just that of the EC. Berlinguer, at the 1976 Berlin Conference, outlined the pan-European strategy of the PCI:

> We will continue to develop our European initiative in many and various directions: on the all-European level, in order to help detente and cooperation; on the West European level, in order to find the broadest meeting points with other left-wing, democratic and progressive forces; and on the level of the European Community in order to make our contribution towards ensuring that the process of integration is democratic and consistent with the interests of the working classes.[6]

At the moment, an essential ingredient in the pan-European strategy of the PCI, the PCF, and the PCE is to work within the EC. This was not always the case. All those parties originally opposed and denounced the EC. The CPSU and the Portuguese Communists remain unremitting opponents of European integration, and the British party played a significant role in the campaign for British withdrawal from the Common Market during the referendum in 1975.

Even so, the main CPs in Southern Europe have, over the years, changed their mind. The Italian and Spanish parties are the most committed to the European Communities and the PCF is the most lukewarm. It accepts the Common Market as a fact of life but exploits powerful Gaullist impulses about preserving French national independence. Although the main parties have various reasons to support the EC, all the major European parties, however, share in common the proclaimed desire to change the character of the EC. Giorgio Napolitano, of the PCI, has set out the directions in which he would like to see the Common Market move, and in terms which many ardent European integrationists would probably accept:

> Yet the Communities (EC) could well serve as a spokesman for Western Europe's vital need for economic independence;

it could favor an *autonomous* and co-ordinated development and support a common resistance to the threat that the present phase of the world crisis will lead the United States to reaffirm and strengthen its supremacy against the countries of capitalist Europe. This is the line for which we fight within the EC.[7]

Together with this obvious desire to weaken the links between the EC and the United States, 'Eurocommunist' pronouncements about the EC are suffused with calls for the 'democratization of the structures and orientations' of the EC (a convoluted way of attacking the Brussels bureaucracy and the capitalist nature of the Community). They call also for the deepening of relations between the EC and the Eastern bloc. The Communist parties of Western Europe see their participation in the EC as helping to foster a dynamic phenomenon—to ease Western Europe as a whole into a more neutral position in the world.

Yet, although the strategic aim of the CPs in Western Europe is to weaken the EC's relationship with the United States, no senior European Communist figure has gone so far as to call for the unification of the EC with Comecon. Instead, the immediate aim is to improve relations between Western and Eastern Europe. This neutral position of the European CPs often leads them into heady speculation about the ability of future CP governments or CP-influenced governments to construct a genuinely independent Western Europe.

This speculation is fueled by the European Communists themselves, whose European pronouncements are replete with assertions about Socialist 'regionalism' and are silent about 'proletarian internationalism'. Carrillo, as would be expected, has been in the forefront of schismatic allusions—the leader, as it were, of the reformation in Eastern Europe: 'For years, Moscow was our Rome. We spoke of the great October Socialist Revolution as if it were *our* Christmas. That was the period of our infancy. Today we have grown up.'[8] *The Economist* has also referred to 'the reformation' analogy in an article on 'Eurocommunism' entitled 'Waiting for Comrade Luther'. Yet it argued, rightly, that 'Spain's Mr. Carrillo and Italy's Mr. Berlinguer have not yet completed that leap of faith to the principles of protestantism. Comrade Luther has not yet arrived'.[9]

Yet, the question remains: how plausible is a future independent, integrated, Western Europe, if it should come increasingly under 'Eurocommunist' rule? The answer must remain: not very plausible at all. First, it is a mistake to imagine that the whole of Western Europe is for the immediate future threatened by Communist or Communist-influenced governments. The Federal Republic of Germany, the Scandinavian nations, the Low Countries and Great Britain would be outside any new regional Communist Western Europe. Hence, if the Communists were to achieve a significant measure of power in Italy, France, and even Spain, then Western Europe would be split. It would not develop, *as a whole*, towards a united, neutral future. France, Italy and Spain might form a southern belt, and West Germany and her immediate neighbours to the north and west, a northern belt, which presumably would still keep its close links with the United States. In other words, to imagine that there would be a general, and systematic Western European turn to neutralism is fanciful. The most likely eventuality, in the event of Communist participation in the governments of southern Europe, is a fractured Western Europe leading to intense economic and political instability. Even economic co-operation would be jeopardized. In the event of Communist participation in the Southern European governments, for example, are the Northern European states likely to assist them economically when they have balance of payments and currency problems? Can we expect a Christian Democratic or even an SPD government in Bonn to come to the aid of the Communist party of France after it insists on nationalizing major banks and industries and suffers a flight of capital? Under the best of circumstances it has been difficult to secure co-operation between democratic governments across state boundaries in Europe even when sister parties are in power. It would appear next to impossible if Communist parties become major partners in the governments of southern Europe.

In addition, the continuing neutrality of an 'Eurocommunist' southern Europe would be open to question. The anti-imperialist and anti-American rhetoric behind the CPs' desire for a neutral Europe could easily get the better of them, particularly if the United States and other western nations are unsympathetic to the new bloc. Furthermore, (as is discussed below) the proclaimed Communist antipathy towards both military blocs, together with complacency about Soviet expansionist impulses, could easily lead to even more cuts in southern European defense spending and the eventual expulsion of US bases. Apart from a hint by Carrillo that a European 'defense force' might sometime be necessary, the CPs of southern Europe seem uninterested in either erecting or sheltering behind a European military capability in order to improve their bargaining position with the Russians. In the event of decreased US military involvement and commitment to Western Europe—virtually an assured feature of Communist rule in southern Europe—then, in the absence of an integrated West European defense build-up, the Soviet Union will become the undisputed dominant military power on the European continent. In such circumstances, it is difficult to foresee a 'Eurocommunist' southern Europe being able to keep, even if it wanted to, its neutrality. At best, it would be 'Finlandized'.

An alternative possibility is that a 'Eurocommunist' Southern Europe could develop alongside a Northern Europe whose centre of political gravity has shifted far to the left. The Labour Party could fall under the complete control of the dominant left wing in its National Executive Committee, and the SPD could, more slowly, move to the extreme left as the present generation of 'Jusos' (Young Socialists) move into positions of power. Even in this eventuality, however, it would be difficult to foresee the emergence of a strong, defensible, integrated, anti-Soviet, 'Socialist' Western Europe. Substantial political differences would still remain between the various Communist parties. Rarely have even Communist parties been able to co-ordinate their international policies without the cement of Soviet hegemony. For instance, Professor Are has pointed out that the PCI attempted to establish a co-ordinating centre for the European Communist parties in 1976, but that the others would not go along with the idea. Furthermore, the Communist parties have done little to co-ordinate their strategy in the European Community.

When the Socialist parties to the north are added into this picture there is likely to be even less agreement. Also, each national party continues to have to deal with different economic problems and cultures that will make a united 'Socialist/Eurocommunist' Western Europe unlikely. Moreover, it is inconceivable that such a general move throughout Europe to the left would result in the maintenance of strong defenses or increased defense integration aimed against the Soviet Union. It is unlikely that all these political developments would congeal together at the same time. In these circumstances, the Soviet Union would be able to exploit this instability and disunity.

The other, even grander, scenario for European political development, which is often suggested, is that of a 'convergence' between a 'Eurocommunist' Southern Europe, and the regimes of Eastern Europe. This 'convergence', it is argued, may already be developing whilst the 'Eurocommunist' parties are still in opposition. It is suggested that the Communist parties of Western Europe—Carrillo's 'pole of reference for the whole working class movement'—are an example and encouragement to the Eastern European regimes to liberalize their systems; and when, and if, the Western Communists achieve power, there will be a natural pan-European coalescence that will draw Eastern and Western Europe together. This, essentially, is the theory of 'infection'—the Western European Communists will 'infect' the Eastern European regimes, both with their 'liberalism' and with their 'national Communism'. As evidence that this historic process is already under way the national roads policy of Romania is cited. Also, the growth of dissidence in Poland, East Germany and Czechoslovakia (where the Charter 77 group is officially supported by many of the Western European Communist parties) is offered as further proof. Presumably, a 'Eurocommunist'-influenced Common Market would be an even greater power magnet for the Eastern Europeans.

Yet, such a 'convergence' flies in the face of the political and military reality in Eastern Europe. The Soviet Union is the major determinant of the parameters of political development there. The events in Poland and Hungary (in 1956) and Czechoslovakia (in 1968) remain a poignant reminder that these parameters are limited and strictly enforced. Mild liberalism (as in Hungary under the Kadar regime) is tolerated as is the repressive form of national communism practiced by Ceausescu in Romania. Even so, no further movement towards either liberalization or independence appears likely from within Eastern Europe. As Professor Schapiro maintains, too excessive a move towards freedom (as the Soviets interpreted the Dubček administration in 1968), or too determined an attempt to break out from the Warsaw Pact (as with the Nagy government in 1956) will, almost certainly, be suppressed by Soviet tanks. Of course, the 'Eurocommunist' presence in Western Europe has evoked from Eastern Europe certain tentative, elliptical responses. The Romanian Party has been the most forthright in defending the Western parties' claims to independence from Moscow.[10] Poland and Hungary have both revealed guarded sympathy for 'Eurocommunism' in their propaganda. The Czechs and the Bulgarians, at the other extreme, have taken the lead in denouncing 'Eurocommunism'. The Bulgarian party leader, Todor Zhivkov, issued an outright denunciation in the pages of *World Marxist Review*:

> This concept, known as 'Eurocommunism', betrays the reactionaries' desires to raise a wall between the brother parties of the Socialist community and those of the West European capitalist countries. . . This ('Eurocommunism') is now one of the main lines of ideological subversion against proletarian internationalism.[11]

In the spectrum of East European responses to 'Eurocommunism' Zhikov's position is likely to be rather more crowded than Ceausescu's. By and large, the East European regimes support the principle of 'proletarian internationalism'. The 'infection' is kept within a tight quarantine.

It is not only the nature of the Soviet military presence and threat, and the economic dependency of the Eastern bloc nations upon Moscow, that causes such obeisance to Soviet wishes. It is also the nature and character of the ruling East European Communist parties themselves. Possessed of only a tiny independent base of their own within their separate nations, they have become, since 1968 at any rate, intermediaries between the Soviet Union and the existing channels of opinion in Eastern Europe. They are, in effect, a cruder and even less representative form of modern Pétainism. Consequently, according to Professor Kriegel, the Russians have no reason to fear any initiative for change from the Communist parties (of Eastern Europe) themselves for when pressure for change comes in Eastern European society, as in Poland, it will come anyway. Certainly, as Professor Schapiro points out, the intriguingly different message of the European parties can affect the populations of Eastern Europe and can give succour to popular centres of resistance, but the ability of non-party groups to act upon their feelings is limited. Also, the regimes of Eastern Europe severely limit, and can be expected to continue to do so in the future, the media coverage available for messages from Rome, Madrid and Paris.

Furthermore, there is room for debate about whether an 'infection' of democratic values and structures—passed from Western to Eastern Europe—would, even in the absence of Soviet control, have a lasting effect. With the exception of Czechoslovakia, no Eastern European nation has a rich and embedded democratic tradition. Thirty or so years of Communist governments do not make it any easier to establish a democratic political system. The European Communist leaders themselves suggest that political change can only take place in their own western nations by respecting the democratic traditions. Giorgio Napolitano refers to the political traditions of his own nation in a typically contrived passage. Italy, he suggests, 'is a highly articulated civil society, . . . rich and autonomous dialectic of diverse, social, ideological and cultural pressures and position'.[12] This presumably means freedom in the Western sense of the concept. The logic of this notion, when applied to Eastern Europe is depressing. It would certainly effectively contain 'infection' in Eastern Europe—circumscribing it by what the Communists would describe as the 'historical conditions'. Irrespective of the strength of Communist governments in Western Europe or of the power of the Soviet Union, the political, social and cultural traditions of the two Europes—East and West—are still fairly distinct. This has implications for democratic development.

THE COMMUNIST PARTIES AND WESTERN DEFENCE

The European parties cannot be considered as resolute or reliable supporters of Western defence. To begin with, they show few, if any, signs of accepting the proposition that the Soviet Union seeks to establish its hegemony over the European continent and is willing to use or threaten to use force to achieve this objective. After all, for them, the Soviet Union and the socialist bloc are forces for 'peace', and it is the US and Western imperialism that is basically aggressive. In interview after interview, the PCI, PCF and PCE leaders, for example, avoid putting themselves on record as suggesting that the Soviet Union may seek to dominate the continent, nor do they express any concern about the rising Soviet military build-up.

When asked what a PCI-controlled government would do in the event of a NATO–Warsaw Pact clash, the PCI leadership repeatedly refuses to commit itself. An interview with Giancarlo Pajetta, head of the PCI's Office of International Relations, was very revealing on this point:

> *Question*: Suppose detente gave way to a military crisis?
> *Answer*: We support negotiations. We always seek to prevent conflict.
> *Question*: But if war breaks out?
> *Answer*: We hope our country would not be involved.
> *Question*: And if it became involved?
> *Answer*: I would hope Italy has the strength to prevent this.
> *Question*: And if the East attacked the West?
> *Answer*: But these are not real considerations, not facts.
> *Question*: Suppose Italy were the subject of an attack by the Warsaw Pact?
> *Answer*: And why should she be attacked? I do not accept the hypothesis. . .[13]

Carrillo has been just as evasive. He has suggested that:

> NATO justifies its existence on the grounds of a possible Soviet attack. . . . But since for more than twenty years no Soviet aggression has taken place and the fundamentally defensive nature of the Warsaw Pact has been confirmed, NATO is becoming a bureaucratic military superstructure in search of a goal with which to justify itself. In the last resort it remains above all an instrument of American political, economic and military control over Europe.[14]

Consequently, the attitudes of the European parties to NATO are generally more hostile than those toward the European Community. Whereas European integration is seen as useful domestically, as well as opening up the possibility for the construction of regional socialism, the NATO connection, particularly under US leadership, offers few advantages.

Historically, of course, the European parties have resolutely opposed NATO. As late as 1972, Berlinguer supported what he termed 'the struggle against the Atlantic Pact' and called for Italy to free itself from 'the bond of subordination . . . to NATO'.[15] The PCF, historically a foe of the Alliance, was (even as late as 1976) still calling for France's withdrawal from its political wing—although in guarded tones: 'France must manifest its will to disengage itself from the Atlantic Bloc by practicing an independent policy in all circumstances.'[16] The PCF, in pursuing its independence strategy, has skillfully used ultra Gaullist nationalist sentiments and rhetoric. The CPGB still echoes the traditional policy of all the NATO CPs and (incidentally) of the CPSU as well: 'Britain should withdraw from NATO, and work for an agreed dissolution of both NATO and the Warsaw Pact and their replacement by an all-inclusive European security system.'[17]

Recently, though, the major Communist parties of southern Europe appear to have had some second thoughts. The PCI was 'not raising the question of Italy's departure from the Atlantic Pact,' and 'was opposed to any other unilateral departure from one bloc or the other'.[18] The PCI leadership went even further, intriguingly so, during the election campaign of 1976 by implying that NATO constituted a shield behind which the Italian party could ensure its autonomy from Moscow.[19] Although the PCF, during the negotiations leading up to the Common Programme, proposed French withdrawal from NATO, it accepted a final version that was ambiguous on this point. The PCF has since suggested that it would be prepared to take part in a government that was not committed to leaving the Alliance. In May of 1977, the PCF also unanimously abandoned its traditional opposition to the French nuclear deterrent. Carrillo has said that he accepts the continuance of American bases in Spain,[20] and in the event of the Spanish Parliament voting to enter NATO, has hinted that the PCE would not organize any serious opposition to it. Even Cunhal, as Machete reports, is not formally opposed to Portugal remaining a member of the Alliance for the present.

Even so, the European Parties' policy regarding NATO remains a fascinating study in ambiguity. The PCI leadership supports Italian membership of NATO in an Alliance predicated upon the notion of a threat from Moscow, yet cannot imagine that the Russians would ever invade. Communists proclaim that the Warsaw Pact is only defensive, that the Soviet Union is a force for peace, yet are willing, in various degrees, to side with an Alliance that believes the opposite; the United States is depicted as aggressive and imperialist, yet, the CP leaderships can envisage taking part in an Alliance under its leadership; the European parties resist anti-Sovietism but accept an Alliance that is anti-Soviet.

Such ambiguity may suit the Southern European Communist parties, which find themselves in a difficult political situation. It allows them to square the circle between internal public opinion (which remains in favour of NATO), their own Stalinist militants (who oppose the NATO involvement) and the Soviet leadership.

Such ambiguity is also an integral part of coalition-making. For instance, in the early seventies, it allowed the PCF much needed flexibility in attempting to arrive at an agreed statement for the Common Programme with the French Socialists: 'The government will make plain its will to move the nation towards independence of any politico-military bloc. The problems posed by the obligations laid on France as a member of the Atlantic Alliance will be reached in that spirit.' Subsequently, Mitterrand could claim that he had persuaded the PCF to accept NATO membership for the time being; and the PCF was free to develop its NATO policy according to the demands of the political situation. In any event, the current ambiguous NATO policy of the PCF represents an ostensible departure from erstwhile outright hostility.

Why the change? One possible explanation is electoral and tactical. Withdrawal from NATO is not popular among the European electorates. As the CPs come within reach of government, this anti-NATO image becomes an electoral albatross which they may feel they need to wrench from around their necks. In fact the first signs of PCI reconciliation to NATO, as opposed to silence on the issue, came, perhaps not coincidentally, during the election campaign of 1976. And it was during the phase of the Common Programme, when electoral considerations were a high priority, that the PCF modified its NATO stance. The PCE, however, has no need to modify its NATO posture, as by backing the status-quo it incurs no electoral odium. The CPGB, on the other hand, can afford to take a rejectionist stance, as it has only a marginal interest in votes.

Its strategic aim is to penetrate the labour movement where there already exists considerably antipathy both to the Alliance and to US nuclear bases in Britain.

Another part of the explanation may lie in the developing strategy of the Communist parties to involve themselves in existing institutions, in order to change them from within—as is the case with the institutions for European integration. Berlinguer insists that the NATO question should be seen in 'dynamic' terms, not in the 'static' viewpoint which conditioned attitudes during the 'cold war'. In two revealing quotes he has outlined this gradualist approach of the PCI, together with a hint that working within NATO, for the time being, might achieve more for the anti-American struggle than leaving: 'One can conceive of our getting out of NATO as a process, as a separation having various stages',[21] and:

> This decisive question of getting free of the bonds of subordination that tie our country to NATO cannot be reduced to a single declaration for or against the military pact. The struggle against the Atlantic Pact will, rather, become more effective the more it is identified with a general movement of liberation of Europe from American hegemony and the gradual surpassing of opposed blocs, up to the point of their liquidation.[22]

Hence, NATO is to be used for more general all-European ends.

The PCI, whose leaders appear to reveal rather more of their thinking about NATO than do other European Communists, has volunteered two further reasons for its shift in policy towards the Alliance. First, Berlinguer may have been sincere when he suggested that NATO can act as a convenient shield behind which the PCI can protect its autonomy from incursions by Moscow. Indeed, it is conceivable that if the PCI continues to assert its independence from Moscow, then NATO participation may become ever more alluring—particularly if the Kremlin were to exert pressure on a post-Tito Yugoslavia. Even so, to use NATO as a weapon in an intra-Communist dispute is a radically new function for the Alliance, one that would fundamentally alter its character and one that, in all probability, the other members of the Alliance would have difficulty supporting.

Second, PCI leaders have suggested[23] that if Italy left NATO, it would upset the military balance between East and West in Europe. Yet, such concern for the military balance is new, and contradicts the PCI's often stated belief that there is no need to fear Soviet military might as the Soviet Union has no aggressive intentions. This interest in the military balance is no long-term guarantee of continuing Italian membership of NATO, as judgements and assessments about force levels can fluctuate. The intriguing implication here may be that if NATO increases its military capabilities sufficiently, then a Communist Italian government would feel free to leave the alliance. Alternatively, the party could also reverse its own decision to remain in the Alliance on other pretexts as well. For instance, on the grounds that it had tried to change the Alliance in a democratic direction, but it still remained under 'German and American hegemony,' or that the Italian government wanted control of NATO installations in Italy, and this had been refused.

CP statements about NATO are contradictory; and CP reasoning about the Alliance is highly questionable. The long and medium-term commitment to NATO of the Western European CPs must remain in doubt as long as they continue to proclaim, on general East–West issues, an anti-imperialist (meaning anti-American and anti-German) ideology, favour a residual neutralism as between the blocs and adhere to a dynamic analysis of the Alliance.

From the Western point of view, a question remains: will Communist participation in the governments of France and Italy weaken NATO? If Italy and France, under Communist promptings, were to withdraw from the Alliance, then NATO would become, essentially, a North American/North European defence pact, relying heavily upon a US/West German accord. Former US Secretary of State Henry Kissinger has suggested that: 'This specter could then be used in other West European countries to undermine what remains of Atlantic cohesion.'[24] Equally important would be the psychological blow. NATO would be seen to be grievously weakened and anti-Soviet resolve would decline. In this atmosphere, the remaining European nations of NATO, including West Germany, might find it irresistible to seek separate deals with the Soviet Union to limit the blow to their security.

The more likely eventuality is that, upon achieving office, the CPs will not press for an immediate withdrawal from the Alliance. Even so, CP governments (or coalitions including the CP), even if they proclaimed their loyalty, would pose serious security problems, not least for the NATO nuclear planning group. There would also be a nagging question mark over the future of US bases; the issue of nuclear bases can easily be separated from generally proclaimed support for the Alliance, as is already the case with Norway and Denmark. There will also be a predisposition in the 'Communist NATO countries' to cut defence budgets: it is unlikely that those who discount the aggressive intentions of the Soviet Union will keep defence spending at the level of those who do not. The pressure which the United States could exert upon a Western European CP government to retain its defence expenditure levels would be minimal.

At a more profound level, NATO, for the first time, would have within its councils member nations whose proclaimed aim is the dissolution of both NATO and the Warsaw Pact, the removal of all foreign bases from European soil, and the resolution of conflict by an all-European security conference. This, too, is the Soviet policy for Europe. With divisions between the European member nations over such fundamental questions of European policy, the political unity of the Alliance is bound to suffer. Also, American public and élite opinion would find it difficult to understand the need to support, in a defence pact, Communist nations against other Communist nations. As Kissinger has suggested: 'The character of the Alliance would become confused to the American people.'[25] Such confusion could lead, at best, to a weakening of American resolve and, at worst, to a growing isolationism based upon an American disenchantment with European politics. American opinion would be more likely to support a truncated NATO than one in which Communist governments participate. Consequently, the entry of Communists into NATO governments would make more likely a potentially fatal double fracture of the Alliance: the first between the northern and southern members, the second between Western Europe and the United States.

Such fissiparous tendencies within the Alliance would destabilize the whole international system and threaten the peace.

Increasing US disaffection with Europe, especially if it led to troop withdrawals or other manifestations of lowered American resolve, would create a power vacuum. In this event, the Soviet Union, although traditionally cautious, might be drawn into the vacuum. Alternatively the remaining non-Communist members of NATO, including France, might in desperation attempt to revive the West European defence pact (this time including a nuclear-armed West Germany) that floundered in the 1950s. Such a move would almost certainly be interpreted by the Soviet Union as provocative.

On issues outside Europe, the European parties strike decidedly anti-Western postures. They, for the most part, go beyond a neutralist stance and echo Soviet policy in their pronouncements on conflicts in Africa, the Middle East and Asia. Also, and significantly, they side with the Soviet Union in its dispute with China. They even refuse to maintain relations with the Chinese. For them, China is a 'socialist' country, but one whose foreign policy is unacceptable because it opposes the Soviet Union and divides the anti-imperialist front. Chinese support for organizations such as the FNLA in Angola is criticized by the European parties, as is Chinese policy in Europe. In 1971, however, Carrillo and four other members of the PCE Executive Committee renewed relations with the Chinese after severing them in the heat of the Sino–Soviet split. Carrillo's purpose, however, was to 'tweak the Soviet nose, not embrace Maoist policy'.

Another indication of the congruity between Moscow and the European parties can be found in the support they gave to Ethiopia after the Soviets shifted their support away from Somalia in the autumn of 1977. Within a short period, the major European parties followed suit.[26] Moreover, the European parties have worked closely with the Soviet Union to promote the destruction of 'Western imperialism', and most of them continue to do so, mounting propaganda drives and helping to train 'anti-imperialist forces' from the non-Western world.[27]

In conclusion, the Communist parties of Western Europe have established for themselves a degree of freedom and national independence through their very selective criticism of Soviet domestic behaviour and their rejection of the Soviet concept of 'proletarian internationalism'. However, so far they have rarely chosen to *exercise* this independence. Their imprecise

European and NATO policies are ambiguous enough not to upset the Soviet Union and, in any event, should be set in the context of their overall support for the Soviet political and economic system, support for the Soviet Union in the schism with China, and support for the Soviet Union in the East–West conflict outside Europe.

It is difficult to view the European parties, in the light of their development to date, as representing a threat to Soviet global policy or interests—either as an incipient 'China' (an anti-Soviet Communist regime), as a potential genuine 'neutral' bloc, or alternatively as a new political force keen upon the defence of Western interests around the world.

THE SOVIET RESPONSE

Seen in this light, it is not surprising that the reaction of Moscow to 'Eurocommunism' has been relatively subdued. The CPSU has kept its response to 'Eurocommunist' criticisms of internal Soviet behaviour on the level of verbal assaults—often elliptical and aimed so widely that no particular party is singled out. Unlike their treatment of the Chinese, the Soviets have not, so far as is known, sought to excommunicate any Western European party by declaring it to be anti-socialist or anti-working class, or by seeking to have them removed from international Communist gatherings. Nor have the Soviets directly attempted to weaken any Western Communist party by any other means—by cutting off funds or by attempting to split them and setting up an alternative CP. On the contrary, as far as can be ascertained, the Kremlin has sought to increase the strength of the Parties financially. Whenever splits occur—as with the schisms within the PCE and the CPGB—they appear to be the work of local disaffected groups (usually unreconstructed Stalinists) rather than the result of direct Soviet interference and encouragement. Even when the Lister faction emerged within the PCE in the late 1960s, Moscow did not lend its full support, nor was this faction able to attract exclusive and unqualified Soviet backing after it split with the PCE.

Of course, the Soviets have to tread carefully. Attempts to sow division between leaders and militants, as was the case recently in Spain, can be counter-productive. Moreover, any attempt to set up a new party could simply divide the Communist forces and weaken basically pro-Soviet CPs. Likewise with the cessation of funding. Consequently, the Soviet reaction to 'Eurocommunism' appears to have remained verbal.

Several of the major European Parties, however, have been at the receiving end of sharp Soviet criticism. This criticism is usually a response to what is considered to be unjustified interference by the CPs in the internal affairs of the Soviet Union. For instance, in January 1977, the Soviet weekly *New Times* carried an article naming, and singling out for criticism, Jean Elleinstein, the deputy director of the PCF's research centre. Elleinstein, the author of a four-volume book on Soviet history, developed a severe critique of Stalinism and even went so far as to suggest that it had its roots in Leninism. He also suggested that liberties had ceased to exist in the Soviet Union by 1922 and chastised the PCF for being slow in criticizing the lack of liberty in the Soviet Union. Elleinstein was denounced by the Soviet Union for behaviour 'totally unbecoming for a person who calls himself a Communist'. Even more severe, and of more importance too, was the Soviet attack upon Santiago Carrillo following the publication of his book, *'Eurocommunism' and the State*. Carrillo's main heresy was not his espousal of democracy and freedoms in Spain, but rather his sharp attack upon the Soviet regime, in particular his suggestion that the Soviet Union is not socialist. The Soviet riposte was directed specifically at Carrillo as an individual. He was depicted as deliberately anti-Soviet: aiming to divide Western parties from the Soviet Union; and playing into the hands of class enemies.[28]

The PCI's altogether more subtle approach to relations with the Soviets leaves it less open to counter-attack. And the PCI has been careful never to suggest that the Soviet Union is not socialist; indeed, Giancarlo Pajetta, a leading PCI spokesman on international affairs, went so far as to criticize Carrillo for suggesting such heresy. Although refusing to question the socialist basis of Soviet society, the PCI continues to reject Soviet treatment of some dissidents and specific acts such as the Warsaw Pact invasion of Czechoslovakia.

By comparison with their sensitivity over criticisms of Soviet life, Leonard Schapiro has pointed out that Moscow is relatively relaxed when it comes to the European parties' espousal of freedoms and pluralism within their own societies. Moscow raises no public objection to the dropping of 'the dictatorship of the proletariat' from Western Communist Party aims, nor to the various general professions by Western CPs in favour of human rights. The communiqué issued after the 'Madrid Summit' in March, 1977 was forthright on the question of 'bourgeois freedoms'. Its open espousal of pluralism, of freedom of thought and religion, obviously disturbed Moscow. Even so, there was no public denunciation of the freedoms passage. Instead, *Pravda* simply omitted the whole of the passage concerned when it belatedly published the text of the communiqué on 7 March. Schapiro notes the Soviets may not be taking the European CPs seriously, remembering their own professions about democracy and pluralism prior to the Bolshevik Revolution and the claims of the East European Communist leaders prior to Soviet control of Eastern Europe after the Second World War.

'Polycentricism' and 'national roads' to Socialism remain sensitive issues in Moscow, particularly as they run counter to the oft stated Soviet theory of 'proletarian internationalism'. Even so, the European parties continue to insist upon their independence from any 'directing centre'. But even on this issue, the Soviet leadership shows signs of some restraint. For instance, the chief Soviet ideologist and top ranking Politburo member, Mikhail Suslov, who led Soviet polemical attacks upon Peking's nationalist deviations in the early 1960s, charged Communist parties who espoused 'national' versions of Marxism with 'opportunism'. While these remarks were carried by TASS in the report of his speech, they were omitted by *Pravda* the following day.[29] Such shifts may reflect some form of internal Soviet debate about the wisdom of attacking the national roads nostrum. Professor Schapiro, however, suggests that it is difficult to accept the validity of speculations of some western scholars about dissension and even disarray among Soviet leaders on the subject of 'Eurocommunism'. Although there may be differences in nuance among Soviet specialists on this subject, the CPSU International Department reflects a unified Politburo policy.

While Moscow clearly has been displeased from time to time with the 'Eurocommunist' parties, it still tries to orchestrate the Parties into its grand strategy. Soviet leaders, historically at any rate, have not taken the view that the advance of power of the European parties is at all times its first strategic priority. Soviet policy, after all, is carried out both on the state-to-state level and the party-to-party level. Moscow seeks to integrate its instruments on both levels to achieve maximum results.

Moscow, for example, may have an acceptable relationship with a given government which the too rapid advance of the domestic Communist party may put in jeopardy. For instance, Soviet support for De Gaulle and his successors just before French elections often annoyed and irritated the PCF leadership. The PCF has been critical of the Soviet Union for placing what it considers to be Soviet State interests in detente ahead of French Party interests. This particular criticism surfaced at the 1976 Berlin Conference when Marchais declared: 'However, we cannot accept any measure which, claiming to be taken in the name of peaceful coexistence, would run counter to the interests of the struggle which we are waging against the might of big business for democracy and socialism.'[30] Also, the local Communist parties may want, for their own reasons, to adopt certain political tactics, such as strikes, which may not fit in with overall Soviet policy.

Also, it is by no means clear that increasing the strength of the local Communist Party is the best possible means for shifting the 'correlation of forces' against the West. That shift may be furthered by Soviet pressure for change (favourable to the Soviet Union) applied directly upon non-Communist parties and governments—part of what Jean-Francois Revel has referred to as 'the totalitarian temptation.' Indeed, a pliant regime which is not officially 'communist' may be preferable to a Communist regime that may cause difficulties.

In short, from the Soviet view, Soviet influence in Europe cannot exclusively be measured by the strength of the European parties; and the Soviets, by operating on both the state-to-state level as well as on the party-to-party level, often cause problems for the European parties. For example, Moscow disapproved of the 1972 Common Programme between the PCF and the Socialists and strongly defended the PCF in the wake of its dissolution (*Pravda*, October 2, 1977). Moscow also appeared originally to have been less than enthusiastic about the Historic Compromise in Italy. It may have thought that the time was not then ripe for Communist participation in a Western government. The fear here may have been that détente might have been jeopardized by too precipitate a change in one of the NATO states.

Yet, the Soviet Union shows every sign of believing that the advance of its interests in Europe is best achieved within the context of the Communist movement, and by Communist parties. Soviet ideologists continue to insist upon this point; and the fact remains that the Communist parties, irrespective of differences with Moscow, cannot possibly possess as many centres of potential opposition to 'Finlandization', or to the presence of Soviet power in Europe, as do the non-Communist parties. This is the main reason why Moscow shows such interest in every nuance of policy emanating from its sister parties. This is the reason why there has been no attempt by the Soviet Union to destroy or weaken the West European Communist parties. Ironically, a process, which at this stage, could be set in train by lavish praise from Moscow.[31]

SOVIET SOURCES OF INFLUENCE

The restrained nature of the Soviet response to the challenges of the Western European Communist parties contrasts with the less restrained response of Moscow to other foreign members of the Communist 'family' who have called into question the authority of the centre. Moscow, of course, has available a battery of sanctions which it can threaten to use in any inter-Communist dispute. It could decide to end formal contacts and the exchange of fraternal delegations. It could deprive the European parties of the moral and financial support of the most powerful socialist party and state. It could even attempt to engineer splits within the European parties and create new Communist parties which would be loyal to its every need. This, however, it has not chosen to do amongst the European parties. Evidently, Moscow does not believe that the situation in Western Europe is serious enough to merit such drastic action. Also, the Soviet leadership has other means open to it to influence the direction of its difficult partners.

One source of influence which the Soviet Union can use to affect the direction of the European Communist leadership is the continuing pro-Soviet loyalty of large sections of the European CPs' rank and file. Each European party has its share of unreconstructed Stalinists (usually the older members) and modern Russophiles. The PCF, for example, has a sizeable pro-Russian activist core, as does the PCI. Every year the major parties, particularly the Italian and French, organize vacation trips and study tours to Russia and the Eastern bloc nations and thousands of party activists and ordinary workers pay part of the cost of these trips.

These trips help to strengthen relations between the ordinary party worker and the Soviet Union and, indeed, are intended to increase the admiration of the party faithful for the social, political and economic accomplishments of Soviet life. It is unlikely that pro-Soviet sentiment will die within the CPs of Western Europe as the older generations are replaced. The extent to which the Soviet Union can exploit this pro-Soviet feeling among the European Communist militants is unclear and unmeasurable. That it remains a source of continuing Soviet influence is not in question.[32] Nor is the ability of Moscow, any time it wishes, to use this reservoir of good will, indeed, devotion, to cause internal political trouble for a recalcitrant national party leadership.

The Soviet Union and its Eastern European allies are also a source of funds for most of the European parties. Although it is impossible to determine the precise extent of this support, or the degree to which the European Parties are dependent on it, it appears to be significant. While the larger parties may now have many *national* sources of support, including subsidies from their governments, the European parties would be seriously handicapped if the Soviets withdrew their subsidies. In point of fact, however, Moscow does not appear to be doing any such thing; although Professor Schapiro notes that at the time of the Madrid Summit the Soviets may have threatened to cut back their subsidies.

The major parties appear to rely financially on the Soviet Union less than they did when they were weaker. Now they appear to receive considerable resources from a dedicated and disciplined party membership, from numerous 'capitalist' enterprises the party owns, and from the municipalities they control. They also appear to be the beneficiaries of business arrangements between Western companies who wish to sell to the Soviet Union and Eastern Europe. Westerners who wish to sell have to work through middle-men who receive large commissions that are subsequently turned over to the party.[33]

However, the Europeans also appear to receive considerable support directly from the Soviet Union and Eastern Europe. The precise techniques for transmitting these funds and the amounts are, of course, carefully guarded secrets. However, occasionally rather startling pieces of evidence appear—for example, Montaldo's analysis of the PCF relation with, and dependence on, a Soviet-owned bank in Paris, or Harold Wilson's and Henry Kissinger's statements that in a twelve-month period, the Soviet Union sent $50–100 million to the Portuguese Communist Party. Overall, by allowing the parties to receive commissions from Western trade with the Soviet bloc, Moscow appears to be increasing its support for the major European parties.

Another lever which the Soviets may be able to pull in order to influence the direction of the Communist parties of Western Europe is derived from the Communist parties' likely dependence upon the Soviet Union if they should come to power. Whether they rule alone or in coalition, there will inevitably be considerable resistance to their rule, particularly if they move to 'transform' their societies too quickly. Communist governments might be tempted to consolidate their control over their societies for fear of being ousted at future elections. In this situation, facing hostility from both their own public and from non-Communist Western Europe, their only major source of support would be the Soviet bloc. If they are to consolidate their power, they will need financial resources and maybe even the threat of military intervention from the Soviet Union to back them up. As has been pointed out, if they ran into balance of payments problems—with weak currencies and a flight of capital—then it is unlikely that the Western financial community will offer aid and trade without economic and political strings that are unacceptable (to the Communists). In this eventuality, too, the governing CPs might prefer to turn eastwards. In such circumstances, continued Soviet goodwill would be of the utmost importance to the local Communists. In a very real sense, the Soviet Union will be in a position to determine whether the local CP could stay in power and surmount its difficulties.

Another possible source of Soviet influence on key European Communists is blackmail, particularly against those who were politically active in the Second World War. Professor Schapiro notes that the CPSU's International Department maintains representatives in various embassies who engage in clandestine pursuits and intelligence gathering. He notes that there has been some conjecture that Moscow has compromising evidence about what he calls Marchais' 'dubious record during the war'. If it has, past Soviet and Communist practice does not indicate Moscow would be reticent about using it. For instance, at the end of the Second World War, the French Communists used this technique to secure co-operation from non-Communist officials and business men who had compromised themselves during the war. They obtained this information from the police files they seized when France was being liberated.[34] Furthermore, the American columnist, Victor Riesel, has maintained that the PCP was able to use police files made available during the 1974 coup to blackmail the then Portuguese Minister of Labour, Captain Costa Martins. Under Martins' tenure, the PCP was able to consolidate its influence on the labour movement.[35]

Finally, Moscow may also have developed its own directly-controlled organization or 'apparat' within the European Parties. Needless to say, information about this type of activity is unavailable. In the past, however, the Soviets did establish their own trusted men in foreign Communist Parties and succeeded in changing the directions and even the leadership of some of these Parties. No doubt the KGB and representatives of the CPSU International Department in Europe display a continuing concern with these matters; but the extent to which they can and are able to manipulate the Parties through these 'agents of influence' is, unfortunately, unknown.

THE INTERNATIONAL BALANCE OF ADVANTAGES

In light of the European parties' *general* support for Moscow, their ambiguous public attitudes towards NATO and European unity, and the sources of influence upon them still open to the Soviet leadership, it cannot be an exaggeration to conclude that Moscow views their growth as an over-all plus in its efforts to shift the correlation of world forces further in its favour. Indeed, Moscow shows little inclination to break with its West European allies and, indeed, regularly praises their over-all contribution to this effort. Furthermore, if the European parties' criticisms of Moscow help them increase their allure within their various societies, the Kremlin may indeed gain something from the public challenges they pose to Moscow.

The increased strength of the European parties can decisively affect the future balance of power in Europe. At its most dramatic, it can help serve to achieve what the Soviets themselves have been unable to do during the past thirty years—namely, to detach Western Europe from the United States without war. Also, the European parties in power can help to prevent the emergence of a united Europe hostile to the Soviet Union. Indeed, Communist participation in the European Community would divide Western Europe. Communists in the governments of Italy or France, or both, could set in train a North/South split. This would have devastating consequences for NATO. If Communists assumed a paramount role in government, the cohesion of NATO would be threatened, as well as its effectiveness. The United States would be forced to exclude the Communist NATO countries from receiving various types of sensitive information—as was the case when Portugal was excluded following PCP participation in the Lisbon government in 1975. In addition, the Communist NATO states, no matter protestations to the contrary, would be seen as less reliable allies in the event of an East/West conflict. This would further reduce the effectiveness (and deterrent value) of the Alliance. Also, as has been discussed, the identity of the Alliance would be damaged and American and non-Communist West European public opinion would begin to question the value of an anti-Soviet alliance that includes governments who share major political assumptions with the Soviet Union. The idea of American, British or West German taxpayers willingly paying for their sons to guard Berlinguer and Carrillo from Soviet tanks is, frankly, difficult to imagine!

The symmetry of the political balance on the European continent would be destroyed. Communist governments would emerge in Western Europe, but pro-Western governments would not appear in Eastern Europe. The European Community would be damaged, but not COMECON. NATO would be weakened, but not the Warsaw Pact. More importantly, the Soviet Union would inevitably emerge as the undisputed major power—politically, militarily and economically—on the European continent.

The result of such a process, irrespective of the Western Communist Parties' wishes, could be to create a psychology of inevitability about growing Soviet power which could lead to each Western European nation seeking a separate settlement with the Soviet Union as part of a developing 'Finlandization' of the Western continent. In this environment, the continuing United States' commitment to Western Europe would obviously be brought into question, not least within the United States itself.

Furthermore, Communist participation in government would probably increase the Soviet ability to obtain credits and technology from Western Europe. It would also tend to reduce the anti-Soviet concerns of the Europeans and make the Soviet Union less frightening and more respectable. It also would enable the European parties to add considerable weight to the Soviet bloc in the Third World and in international forums.

Finally, the increased strength of the European parties may provide Moscow with an additional political–military asset in the midst of Western Europe. While there may be a significant difference between the pre- and early post-Second World War ability of the Soviet Union to manipulate the European parties, and the major non-governmental organizations the latter control, the European parties still may be willing to support Soviet political–military objectives.

Although it was impossible in the course of the study to determine the capabilities of the parties to engage in espionage, sabotage and other covert operations, Rui Machete pointed out that the Portuguese party, at least, would still be able to function quite well in the underground. In addition, control of sizeable resources and institutions, such as municipalities and major sections of organized labour, may give the parties significant assets that would affect the distribution of international power in unstable conditions, or in the event of war.

However, there are also risks for the Soviet Union in the increased strength of the European parties or their entry into government. To begin with, they may become 'awkward dependents' in need of financial and perhaps military support. Moscow, however, has shown little reluctance to underwrite Communist regimes and parties throughout the world as long as they refuse to side with the Chinese or go off on their own, as was the case in Yugoslavia. Massive Soviet support to Cuba and Vietnam are precedents. While it sometimes may be expensive, Moscow has been willing to pay the price—especially for strategically significant allies.

Second, the Soviet leaders may not have wished to upset detente. Unquestionably, Moscow has not wanted to alarm the US and other members of NATO by *dramatically* upsetting the Alliance, and the too-rapid assumption of power by a major European party could have had that effect. Hence, the Soviets may have been attempting to slow down the advance of their European allies, particularly in France and Italy, lest this endanger detente or lead to an anti-Soviet reaction amongst Western states. French re-entry into the NATO organization, or a rapid increase in US and Western European defense spending could form part of this kind of reaction. However, Moscow, as far as is known, did not oppose the PCP's entry into government—although it may have cautioned restraint when the PCP attempted what can be described as a 'coup' in 1975. And in the January, 1978, Italian government crisis, Moscow criticized the Carter Administration's public opposition to PCI entry into the government and through its press advocated PCI participation in the government. Hence, under what it deems the correct circumstances, Moscow is not opposed to increasing Communist strength and control of government.

A third problem for the Soviet Union with the increasing influence of the 'Eurocommunist' parties is the danger of 'infection' in Eastern Europe and the Soviet Union. As has been pointed out, Moscow appears to be particularly sensitive about the European Parties' criticism of the Soviet system. The criticisms of the Soviet Union by European Communists, of course, carry more weight than those of the non-Communist West, especially when they penetrate into the Soviet bloc. However, as Schapiro and others point out, Soviet and Communist governments do not rule Eastern Europe by virtue of ideology. Moscow may at some point decide that the disadvantages of the Europeans' criticism outweigh their contribution to furthering Soviet foreign policy aims, and this may precipitate a rupture. Moscow still seems able and willing to live with this risk.

The most serious threat that the European parties could conceivably present to the Soviet Union would involve their collectively attempting to mobilize the resources of the Western continent and entering into an alliance with the rest of Europe and the United States and China, or both. Such a development would pose an overwhelming threat to the Soviet Union, because it would inevitably entail the emergence of a unified Western Europe, more anti-Soviet than it is today, and capable of bringing enormous economic and even military pressure to bear in the struggle—a struggle made more fearsome by the ideological vigour of converted anti-Soviets. This admittedly very remote possibility presumably accounts for Soviet concern about the emergence of a united Europe, even though it might be 'socialist'.[36] Presumably what upsets the Kremlin is not a neutral, 'socialist' Europe (that would be a net international gain) but a united 'socialist' (or indeed capitalist) Europe that would be able to develop real political, economic and military cohesion and be able to ally with other major power centres such as the United States or China.

The danger of genuinely independent Communist parties controlling the skilled manpower and resources of large parts of the European continent, possibly banding together with a far-left Labour party and SPD in government, attracting the Eastern European parties and allying with the United States and the Chinese, must surely be a scenario Moscow wishes to avoid. However, it is also an extremely remote possibility. In the short and medium run, it is highly unlikely. The European parties are far from united in anything anti-Soviet, except their assertions of independence from Moscow. It is not easy to imagine that these nationalist parties could unite their power, make a deal with the Federal Republic of Germany, and secure the co-operation of the United States. Much more likely, southern European states under Communist rule would bring about enormous instability in Western Europe which, if it did not result in war, would leave the Continent 'Finlandized'.

From the US (and the non-Communist European) perspective, the changes in the European parties are intriguing. Should they continue to evolve in a democratic direction and change character, join the democratic consensus, and disentangle themselves from the Soviet Union's foreign policy not only in Europe but throughout the world, they could, of course, be an important asset to the West. They would add their weight, and that of the important non-governmental actors they control, to the solution of the economic and social problems of Europe and the Atlantic world. They might also solidify Western defense efforts simply by removing the threat that pro-Moscow forces assuming a major role in government now pose to the Atlantic Alliance. But in the unlikely eventuality that the parties evolve in this way, they will probably split. The result of a series of such organic splits might create an intriguing new political terrain on the left. Relatively small pro-Moscow factions would be consigned again to the outer fringes of European politics; and the energy, organization and vitality of the main Party machinery would be harnessed to the democratic left in Europe.

As this study has shown, however, the evolution of the parties so far has not proceeded to this point. While there have been some changes in ideology, alliance patterns in domestic politics, and possibly in the case of the Spanish party some rethinking of 'democratic centralism,' they do not lead to the conclusion that the parties have become parties 'like others' in Europe, genuinely participating in and seeking to improve the democratic order. Moreover, given their ideological affinity and the continuing thrust of their foreign policy, they still remain a net advantage to the Soviet Union. While it may be possible to exploit the changes that have taken place, and by skillful diplomacy to divide them further from the Soviet Union, their increased strength remains an important net disadvantage to the West. The entry of the European parties into positions of power can, in the long term, only be a major setback for the West.

Notes

INTRODUCTION

1. Rt. Hon. Dr. David Owen, 'Communism, Socialism, and Democracy,' The Hugh Anderson Memorial Lecture, November 18, 1977, London: The Cambridge Union Society, 1977.
2. The International Labor Program of Georgetown University in Washington, D.C. assists trade unions and educational institutions to organize international affairs programs. To this end, it co-operates with unions, labour centres, universities, and other educational organizations in the U.S. and abroad.

    The National Strategy Information Center (NSIC) is a non-partisan institution organized to conduct educational programs on international security affairs. With offices in New York and Washington, D.C., NSIC exists to encourage an understanding of strategy and defense issues on the grounds that, in democracies, informed public opinion is necessary to ensure a viable Western defense system.

I THE STRENGTH OF COMMUNIST PARTIES IN WESTERN EUROPE

1. These parties would include the West German FDP, the British Liberals, and the forces of the 'Lecanuet' centre in France.

    The 'Socialist International' is the international organization of Socialist and Social Democratic parties.
2. 'A European Community of Political Parties,' *The Economist*, December 31, 1977, p. 56.
3. These estimates are based on assumptions that Spain would be allocated 53 new seats and Portugal 20 new seats, as indicated by the size of

their populations, and that the PCE would win five of Spain's seats, and the PCP three of Portugal's, based upon their percentage of the vote in their nations' most recent elections.

4. These figures include the results of the first round of balloting in the March, 1978 French Assembly elections. The first-round results are a better reflection of real support for a party than are the results of the second round, in which some candidates withdraw in favour of others.

5. George Urban, 'A Conversation With Altiero Spinelli—Eurocommunism, Again', *Encounter*, January, 1978, p. 8. In this interview Spinelli also explains that he was elected to the Chamber of Deputies in 1976 after the PCI asked him to run as an independent with their support.

6. Even so, Communist parties, no matter how large, consider themselves as the 'vanguard' of the 'proletariat'.

7. For a number of years estimates of Communist party membership appeared annually, until the US government decided to discontinue this series in 1974, in a publication of the Bureau of Intelligence and Research of the US Department of State entitled *World Strength of Communist Party Organizations* (Washington, DC: US Government Printing Office). A publication of the Hoover Institution on War, Revolution, and Peace entitled *Yearbook on International Communist Affairs* (Stanford, Cal.: Hoover Institution Press); and *The Europa Yearbook* (London: Europa Publications Limited), remain sources of Communist Party statistics.

8. Giuseppe Are, in the paper prepared for this study, listed the PCI membership as having increased (based upon *Almanacco PCI*) each year since, and including, 1972 as follows: 1,513,956; 1,611,073; 1,643,716; 1,711,402; 1,794,008. He also states that PCI membership between 1971 and 1976 rose by 18.77% more than did the Italian population. The PCI also recruits amongst Italian citizens residing abroad (primarily 'guest workers'); among this group PCI membership, according to Are, increased 47.6% between 1971 and 1976.

9. See the monthly journal of the French Communist Party, *Cahiers du Communisme*, February/March, 1978, p. 147. Annie Kriegel, in research prepared for this study (and in published works), has challenged the validity of PCF claims about membership. In any event, though, she does concur with the general thesis that PCF membership has increased considerably from 1961 to the present day, and is still growing.

10. Eusebio Mujal-Leon, in his paper for this study, suggests that the figure for PCE membership in 1977 was closer to 200,000. A U.S. Congressional study suggests 100,000 as a 'judicious' estimate; see Foreign Affairs and National Defense Division, Congressional Research Service, Library of Congress, *A Report on West European Communist Parties*, submitted by Senator Edward W. Brooke to the Committee on Appropriations, United States Senate, June, 1977 (Washington, DC: US Government Printing Office, 1977) (hereafter cited as 'Brooke study'), p. 121.

11. Figures of membership for selected CPs are: West Germany (DKP), 40,000; Great Britain (CPGB), 28,651; Austria (KPO), 25,000; Sweden (UPK), 17,000; Belgium (PCB) 10–12,500; Netherlands (CPN), 10–12,000; Denmark (DanKP), 7–8,000; Norway (NKP), 2,500; Greece

(KKE), 28,000. Source, Brooke Study, *op. cit.*, p. 4, except for the CPGB figures, which are CPGB Central Organization Department figures for 1975–6, carried in *The British Communist Party*, Socialist Worker Training Series, No. 3 (London: Socialist Worker Printers and Publishers, Ltd., 1977), p. 23.

12. Neil McInnes *The Communist Parties of Western Europe* (London: Oxford University Press, 1975), p. 37. McInnes provides us with an intriguing and detailed analysis of PCF 'fluctuations' in membership in the period leading to 1974: pp. 36–7.

13. *Ibid.*, p. 37.

14. For a 1966 survey see Annie Kriegel, *The French Communists: Profile of a People* (Chicago: University of Chicago Press, 1972), pp. 70–1. Also listed in McInnes, *op. cit.*, p. 63.

15. Michelle Perrot and Annie Kriegel, *Le Socialisme Français et le Pouvoir* (Paris: Etudes et Documentation Internationale, 1966), pp. 207–8. Cited in McInnes, *op. cit.*, p. 67.

16. *Ibid.*, p. 67.

17. The PCI at the leadership level (especially as Parliamentary candidates) has recently attracted upper class and upper-middle class types. A former NATO General ran on the Party's lists for the Assembly in the 1976 national election.

18. Brooke study, *op. cit.*, p. 80. In 1976, 40% of the delegates to the PCF's Federations were under 30. The figure for 1966 was 10%.

19. In the Policy Statement of 1977, the CPGB states: 'Major improvements in the position of women under capitalism can be won, . . . but the conditions for their full liberation can only be achieved as socialism is built. . . .'. And, 'the continued subjugation of women in their *personal* relationships . . . would limit their potential role in building a socialist society' (emphasis added). Communist Party of Great Britain, *The British Road to Socialism—Programme of the Communist Party* (London, 1978), pp. 59–60.

20. Electoral programme for the 1976 national elections. Reprinted in *L'Unita*, Rome, May 16, 1976; cited in Brooke study, *op. cit.*, p. 59.

21. Enrico Berlinguer, 'Por un Governo si Svolta Democratica,' Rome, 1972, p. 73, cited in Neil McInnes, *op. cit.*, p. 52.

22. Kriegel, *The French Communists . . .*, *op. cit.*, p. 59; and *Le Monde*, Paris, February 23, 1973 and March 10–11, 1974, cited in McInnes, *op. cit.*, p. 50.

23. CPGB figures for 1975–6 show the following membership percentage according to region: Scotland, 25%; London, 16%; North West, 12%; Wales, 6%. All these figures, particularly those for Scotland and Wales, are significantly larger than the population of these regions as a percentage of the national total. See the Socialist Workers Training Series, *op. cit.*, p. 23.

24. The PCP leader A. Cunhal claimed that in September, 1976, 59% of the Party was made up of 'blue collar' workers, 20% of 'white collar', and 13% 'agricultural'. *Report of the Central Committee to the Eighth PCP Congress*, p. 402. Machete, in his paper prepared for this study, agrees that in the rural areas the PCP does draw some strength from

agricultural workers who do not own land.

25. Calculations based on PCF statistics for 1966 indicate 'agricultural' membership of the Party (farm labourers and small farm owners) to be 9.76% of the total. See Annie Kriegel, *The French Communists* . . . , *op. cit.*, pp. 70–71.

26. Guy Hermet, *Los Comunistas en España* (Paris: Ruedo Iberico, 1972), p. 40.

27. See Santiago Carrillo, '*Eurocommunism*' *and the State* (London: Lawrence and Wishart, 1977), pp. 27–33.

28. McInnes, *op. cit.*, p. 57.

29. Small-party popular votes can go up in Britain, both as a total and as a percentage of the national total, according to the number of candidates fielded. The CPGB rarely puts up more than 100 candidates out of a possible 625. Even in the inner-city areas of England, it tends to run well behind the National Front.

30. The CPGB candidate, Jimmy Reid, was a particularly powerful local trade union leader who achieved much, often sympathetic, media coverage after his successful leadership of a workers' sit-in at Upper Clyde Shipbuilders in 1971. He has subsequently joined the Labour Party.

31. See, particularly, David E. Butler and Donald E. Stokes, *Political Change in Britain* (New York: St. Martin's Press, 1974).

32. Figures are: W. Germany, 0.3%; Britain, 0.01%; Austria, 1.0%; Sweden, 4.8%; Belgium, 3.2%; Netherlands, 4.5%; Denmark, 4.2%; Switzerland, 2.2%; Norway, 11.2%; Iceland, 18.3%; Luxembourg, 10.4%; and Eire, 0.4%. Finland (19.0%) is excluded from the overall calculation. Adapted from figures in *The Europa Yearbook*, 1976.

33. Mujal estimates the Spanish figure at 1.7 million.

34. The Spanish figure (for the PSOE and PSP) is estimated at 6,000,000. Brooke study, *op. cit.*, p. 4.

35. The results of the 1948 election have been omitted because the Communists and Socialists ran together and it is impossible to disentangle the votes for the separate parties.

36. From 82.5% in the 1968 sample to 67.4% in the 1975, according to Professor Are's paper for this study.

37. Are refers to a 1975 survey which illustrates this point. Electors, who displayed a political preference, break down (socially) as follows: (1) 'Property-owners, professionals, and government officials' (25%–PCI; 36.3%–CD). (2) 'small entrepreneurs, technicians, teachers' (27.3%–PCI; 30.5%–CD). (3) 'skilled industrial workers' (39.1%–PCI; 32.4%–CD). (4) 'unskilled workers' (40.7%–PCI; 31.4%–CD). (5) 'farmhands, labourers, other unskilled workers not covered in (4)' (43.8%–PCI; 38.8%–CD).

38. The regions where the PCI made the most striking advances were: the industrial North West (Piedmont, Liguria, Lombardy)—an increase of 8.17% to 33.73% of the vote, and in the North and Lazio—an increase of 8.36 to 36.84%, according to Professor Are, in his paper for this study.

39. The regions where the PCF vote exceeded its national average in the 1973 elections were: Limousin, Languedoc–Roussillon, Provence–Côte

d'Azur, Picardie, Région parisienne, Nord, Haute-Normandie, Champ-
agne–Ardennes, and Centre.

40. Calculated from Kriegel, *The French Communists* ... , *op. cit.*, pp. 70–71,
and McInnes, *op. cit.*, p. 71.

41. It has been estimated that whereas the PCF picked up 37% of the
'workers' vote in 1973, the Gaullists achieved 21%. McInnes, *op. cit.*,
p. 72.

42. The PCE received less than 5% of the vote in 22 provinces, between
5% and 10% in 21 provinces, and over 10% in only 8 provinces.

43. The term 'front' should not be confused with the term Communists
use for various types of alliances with other parties, such as 'Popular
Front,' 'National Liberation Front', etc.

44. The twenty-one conditions for formal admission to the Communist International laid down in 1920 specifically stated (Condition 9) that parties
were obligated to work in this fashion in non-Communist organizations.
The 'noyaux' were to be completely subservient to the directives of
the Party. For the twenty-one conditions see Helmut Gruber, *International
Communism in the Era of Lenin—A Documentary History* (Garden City, New
York: Anchor Books, 1972), pp. 241–6.

45. CPGB, *The British Road* ... , *op. cit.*, p. 57.

46. For a major example, see Carrillo, *op. cit.*, which deals at length with
this question.

47. One of the few attempts to assess Communist Party strategy and power
in front organizations can be found in a French best seller, Jean Montaldo's
La France Communiste (Paris: Albin Michel, 1978).

48. Most observers believe that shortly after the Second World War, the
major trade union centres in France and Italy fell under the control
of Communist Parties subservient to Moscow. Some writers now differ
on the extent of present Communist Party control of the CGT and
the CGIL. See Andre Barjonet, *La CGT* (Paris: Seuil, 1968); the article
by Gerard Adam, 'Elements D'Analyse Sur les Liens Entre Le PCF
et la CGT,' *Revue Francaise de Science Politique*, Juin, 1968, pp. 524–39;
the debate between Gerard Adam and Jean Ranger, 'Les Liens Entre
le PCF et la CGT—Elements D'Un Debat', *Revenue Francaise de Science
Politique*, Fevrier, 1969, pp. 182–7; and Jean-Daniel Reynaud, 'Trade
Unions and Political Parties in France: Some Recent Trends', *Industrial
Relations Review*, January, 1975, pp. 208–26. Walter Kendall in *The Labor
Movement in Europe* (London: Allen Lane, 1975), argues that the CGT
and CGIL are still controlled by the French and Italian Communist
parties; and the French journals *Les Etudes Sociales et Syndicales* and *Est
et Ouest* provide detailed information to indicate that the CGT and
CGIL are still controlled by Communist parties that remain basically
loyal to Moscow. For an example of a commentator who believes that
the CGIL is no longer an instrument of the Italian Communist party,
see Peter R. Weitz, 'Labour and Politics in a Divided Movement',
Industrial and Labor Relations Review, January, 1975, pp. 226–43.

49. Jean Montaldo, *Les Finances du PCF* (Paris: Albin Michel, 1977).

50. Michael A. Ledeen, *Italy in Crisis*, The Washington Papers, Vol. 5,
No. 43 (Beverly Hills, California: Sage Publications, 1977). See also

Michael Ledeen and Claire Sterling, 'Italy's Russian Sugar Daddies', *New Republic*, February 12, 1976. Unfortunately these accounts do not provide specific evidence to substantiate the contention.

51. Communist union leaders almost never discuss fraternal financial assistance publicly, but Cipriana Garcia, one of the leaders of the Workers' Commissions, for example, thanked 'the peoples of Europe and of the World for their solidarity in this crucial hour of our history. The Workers' Commissions express their appreciation to the WFTU for its efforts in support of the extension of this international assistance to our people in their battle to conquer their legitimate rights and their freedom'. Pedro Rubio and Venko Kraitchev, 'Interview With Cipriano Garcia', *World Trade Union Movement*, May, 1976, p. 21.

52. Fletcher School of Law and Diplomacy professor/columnist John Roche has a photostat of a telegram from the Soviet Bank for Foreign Trade to a Lisbon bank transferring $28,570 to the Intersindical. See his 'The Portuguese Labyrinth II', *King Features*, August 26, 1975. Moreover, in a rare acknowledgement of organizational assistance, an East German labour leader stated that his organization has given the Portuguese unions 1 million escudos, and has promised additional aid for union buildings, duplicating machinery, and so forth. 'Voice of the GDR', August 2, 1974 (BBC, SWB, EE/4669/A1/1).

53. Wilson maintained that Moscow was sending £48 million (then approximately $100 million per year) into Portugal. *Washington Post*, September 6, 1975. Kissinger estimated that it was only $50 million in a 12-month period. *New York Times*, April 18, 1975.

54. Neil McInnes, for example, argues that in their attempt to control front organizations, the parties are frequently co-opted and certainly are not able to manipulate the CGT and CGIL. See McInnes, *op. cit.*, pp. 8–17.

55. Immediately after the war Communist officials, both in government and in the unions, tried to get workers to rebuild the shattered European economies and refused to support large wage increases. By 1946, however, many workers started to engage in 'wild-cat' strikes against these 'Stakhonovite' tactics.

56. In the Portuguese party's attempts at a coup in October–November, 1975, for example, the Intersindical played a significant role. The PCP, however, did not call for allout union support, as this would have led to civil war.

57. Cited in *The Times*, London, October 15, 1977, p. 4.

58. Cited in Stephen Haseler, *The Death of British Democracy* (London: Elek Books, 1976), p. 125.

59. The CPGB does, however, control *regions* of certain unions, for instance, the South Wales and Scottish areas of the Mineworkers. The CPGB also controls the Scottish TUC.

60. Surprising pro-Soviet statements are regularly made by some leading British trade unionists, both at home and on regular visits to Eastern-bloc countries. For a detailed summary of these statements, see the *Daily Telegraph*, London, February 4, 1977, p. 1; and *The Times*, London, February 4, 1977, p. 2.

61. John F. Kennedy, *Public Papers of the President, 1961–1963* (Washington, DC: US Government Printing Office, 1962, 1963, 1964), p. 334 ff.; cited in Richard J. Walton, *Cold War and Counter-revolution: The Foreign Policy of John F. Kennedy* (New York: Viking Press, 1972), p. 55.

62. Kennedy, *op. cit.*, p. 304ff.; cited in Walton, *op. cit.*, p. 52.

63. Walter Laqueur, 'The Specter of Finlandization', *Commentary*, New York, December, 1977. See also, Adam M. Garfinkle, '"Finlandization": A Map to a Metaphor' (Foreign Policy Research Institute: Philadelphia, 1978).

64. Michel Crozier, in Michel J. Crozier, Samuel P. Huntington, and Joji Watanuki, *The Crisis of Democracy* (New York: New York University Press, 1975) p. 11.

2   The Communist Parties and Domestic Policies

1. See *L'Unità*, Rome, July 1, 1976.

2. He said: 'But while it (the working class) everywhere goes through substantially the same training school for victory over the bourgeoisie, the labor movement of each country affects this development after its own manner ... and the specific country, according to the peculiarities of its politics, economics, culture, national composition, its enemies. ...' Quoted by Jay Lovestone, 'Eurocommunism—Roots and Realities', *AFL–CIO Free Trade Union News* (Washington, DC), June–July, 1977, p. 2.

3. Rt. Hon. David Owen, 'Communism, Socialism, Democracy', (London: Cambridge Union Society, November 18, 1977), pp. 5–6.

4. Eric Hobsbawm, *The Italian Road to Socialism: An Interview With Giorgio Napolitano of the Italian Communist Party* (New York: Lawrence Hill, 1977), p. 9.

5. Interview with Luigi Longo in *Corriere della Sera*, Milan, December 30, 1977.

6. See, for example, Georges Marchais, *Le Defi Democratique* (Paris: Grosset, 1973), and the analysis in Annette Eisenberg Stiefbold, *The French Communist Party in Transition* (New York: Praeger, Special Studies, 1977), pp. 91–3. On the PCI see Don Sassoon, ed., *The Italian Communists Speak For Themselves* (Nottingham: Spokesman, 1978).

7. Communist Party of Great Britain, *The British Road to Socialism—Programme of the Communist Party*, (London, 1978), p. 25. (Emphasis added)

8. Ronald Tiersky, *French Communism, 1920–1972* (New York: Columbia University Press, 1974) p. 44.

9. For amplification, see Eusebio Mujal-Leon, 'The International and Domestic Evolution of the Spanish Communist Party', in Rudolph L. Tokes, ed., *Eurocommunism and the Age of Detente* (New York: New York University Press, forthcoming).

10. PCI Statutes, p. 12.

11. CPGB, *The British Road ...*, *op. cit.*, p. 25.

12. George Urban, 'Communism With An Italian Face? A Conversation With Lucio Lombardo Radice', *Encounter*, May, 1977, pp. 18, 22. Radice is not in the central leadership of the PCI. Even so, as one of the Party's deputed spokesmen to the West, his views are of great significance. On the PCF's views, see Stiefbold, *op. cit.*, pp. 49–58 and 68–70.

13. McInnes, *op. cit.*, p. 97.

14. Marcel Servin, in *Cahiers du Communisme*, June–July, 1954, p. 731.

15. Antonio Gramsci, *L'Ordine Nuovo, 1919–20* (Turin: Einaudi, 1955), p. 99.

16. The following section on the PCI apparatus is drawn almost exclusively from Professor Are's analysis prepared for this study. For a less up-to-date but comprehensive analysis of the PCF see Annie Kriegel, *The French Communists: Profile of a People* (Chicago: University of Chicago Press, 1972), especially pp. 187–307.

17. McInnes, *op. cit.*, p. 111.

18. Kriegel, in her analysis for this study, pointed out that Marchais, in the same speech, derided an alternative system of 'election' by saying that 'With such a system, which would lead to the abolition of the commission on candidacy in actual fact, *chance* would decide whether such or such would be elected an official, since two or three marginal votes would be sufficient to dismiss an extremely capable candidate.'

19. Professor Are's paper for this study has a detailed survey, region by region, of the sections of the PCI. In his paper Rui Machete lists the various functions of the PCP cells. He says: 'It is a fundamental concern of the party leaders that the members should be organized in active cells'.

20. For details of the PCF's central record keeping apparatus, see Kriegel, *op. cit.*, pp. 229–232.

21. PCI Statutes, Article 52.

22. For example, in the last national election to the Italian parliament, 87% of those PCI candidates who were not returned had not offered themselves for election (often at the party's behest). In the DC, the same figure was only 49%. Professor Are points out that a similar pattern can be seen in the previous two elections.

23. For recent examples of what has been a recurring phenomenon in the Communist experience, see Alain de Sedouy and Andre Harris, *Voyage a L'Interieur du Partie Communiste* (Paris: Seuil, 1975), and Vivian Gornick, *The Romance of American Communism* (New York: Basic Books, 1977).

24. Irving Howe, 'Something New Under the Sun,' *Dissent*, Winter, 1978, p. 27. Another American scholar, Robert Putnam, has suggested that PCI electoral strategy and policy are dictated by rational interests which lock them into the democratic mainstream. See 'Italian Foreign Policy: The Emergent Consensus', in Howard R. Penniman, ed., *Italy at the Polls* (Washington, DC: American Enterprise Institute, 1977).

25. Hobsbawm, *op. cit.*, pp. 46–7. (Emphasis added).

26. Cited in Hobsbawm, *op. cit.*, p. 8. (Emphasis added).

27. There is a none-too-stifled echo of Lenin here. Conscious of the need to ensure a broad *social* alliance between the 'proletariat' and a suspicious peasantry, he reversed the economic policy of the young Bolshevik state and introduced 'The New Economic Policy'.

28. *The Economist*, November 12–18, 1977, p. 48.
29. Arnold Hottinger, 'The Rise of Portugal's Communists', *Problems of Communism*, July–August, 1975, p. 3.
30. Boris Kidel, 'Marchais v. Mitterrand', *New Statesman*, October 14, 1977, p. 497.
31. Before the Second World War, the CPGB consistently attempted to gain affiliation to the Labour Party and was rejected.
32. CPGB, *The British Road* . . . , *op. cit.*, pp. 23, 24.
33. *Ibid.*, p. 28.
34. Sydney Bidwell, Chairman of the 'Tribune Group' of Labour MP's (1976–77) argued for a fusion of the two parties in an article in the Communist Party daily *Morning Star*, June 28, 1977, p. 2.
35. Denis Healey, ed., *The Curtain Falls: The Story of the Socialists in Eastern Europe* (London: Lincolns-Praeger, 1951), p. 6.
36. CPGB, *The British Road* . . . , *op. cit.*, p. 57.
37. Jean-Francois Revel, *The Totalitarian Temptation* (Garden City, NY.: Doubleday, 1977), pp. 265–6 (parentheses added).
38. Hobsbawm, *op. cit.*, p. 11.
39. For an example, see Robert Moss, 'The Specter of Eurocommunism,' *Policy Review*, Washington, DC., Summer, 1977, p. 18.
40. This refers to Télé-Monte Carlo. The PCI was keen on enforcing clause 40 of a recent Italian law restricting material broadcast into Italy from abroad. See Michael A. Ledeen, *Italy in Crisis*, The Washington Papers, Vol. 5, No. 43 (Beverly Hills, Cal.: Sage Publications, 1977), pp. 50–3; and Revel, *op. cit.*, especially Chapter 6.
41. For a fuller account of this episode, see Joseph Godson, 'Why the Russians Saw Red Over the Venice Biennale', *The Times*, London, November 12, 1977; Ledeen, *op. cit.*, pp. 50–53; and Michael A. Ledeen, 'Eurocommunists Exposed', *The New Republic*, March 26, 1977.
42. See Giacomo Sani, 'The PCI on the Threshold', *Problems of Communism*, November–December, 1976, p. 30.
43. Joint Statement, PCI and PCF, November 17, 1975, published in Sassoon, *op. cit.*, p. 67.
44. *L'Humanité*, December 23, 1970.
45. Communist Party of Great Britain, *The Communist Party Programme: The British Road to Socialism, Draft for Discussion* (London: CPGB, 1977), Item 1490. (The latter part of the passage was eliminated in the final version of the Party Programme.)
46. *Ibid.*, Item 1770 (emphasis added).
47. Urban, *op. cit.*, p. 18.
48. Santiago Carrillo, *'Eurocommunism' and the State*, (London: Lawrence and Wishart, 1977), quoted in *The Economist*, November 5–11, 1977, p. 63.
49. Text of remarks by Carrillo at a seminar at The Transnational Institute, Washington, DC., November, 1977, reprinted in *In These Times—The Independent Socialist Weekly*, Chicago, December 21–27, 1977. See also Carrillo, *'Eurocommunism' and the State*, *op. cit.*, pp. 76, 100.
50. CPGB, *The British Road* . . . , *op. cit.*, p. 57.
51. Juan Diz (Manuel Azcarate), 'Libertades Politicas y Socialismo', *Alkarrilketa*, Paris, II, No. 2, p. 13.
52. Urban, *op. cit.*, p. 18.

53. From the electoral program of the PCI for the 1976 parliamentary elections, *L'Unità*, Rome, May 18, 1976.
54. From *The Common Programme*, 1972, published in *Keesing's Contemporary Archives, 1971–1972* (Bristol: Keesing Publications, Ltd., 1972), p. 55.
55. *Christian Science Monitor*, September 20, 1977.
56. Cited in Hugh Thomas, 'Señor Carrillo's Schism', *Encounter*, October, 1977, p. 65.
57. There is also a lively debate within the Socialist International about relations with the West European CPs. See Harold Wilson, 'Eurocommunism and the Western Alliance', (London: Labour and Trade Union Press Service, November, 1977), and British Foreign Minister Owen's speech, previously cited. See also Stephen Haseler, 'The Collapse of the Social Democrats', *Commentary*, December, 1977.
58. Carrillo at The Transnational Institute, *op. cit.*, p. 2.
59. See the previously cited Longo interview in *Corriere della Sera*, Milan, December 30, 1977.
60. Carrillo at The Transnational Institute, *op. cit.*, p. 2.
61. 'The Party Program as Adopted by the Congress—I', *The Current Digest of the Soviet Press*, December 6, 1961, p. 14. Napolitano echoes this view, typically less directly, in his own analysis of the theoretical distinctions between the Marxism of the PCI and Social Democracy. He suggests that Communists wish to carry out 'substantial changes in the power relationships between the classes', Hobsbawm, *op. cit.*, p. 29. This, according to Napolitano, distinguishes PCI thinking from that of social democracy.
62. Neil NcInnes, *Eurocommunism*, The Washington Papers, Vol. 4, No. 37 (Beverly Hills, Cal.: Sage Publications, 1976), p. 12.
63. For a detailed and typical list of the composition of the 'intermediate strata' see CPGB, *The British Road . . .*, *op. cit.*, p. 21.
64. On this, see V. I. Lenin, *Two Tactics of Social-Democracy in the Democratic Revolution* (New York: International Publishers, 1935 and 1963), pp. 70, 71, 73; Alfred G. Meyer, *Leninism* (Cambridge, Mass.: Harvard University Press, 1957), pp. 123–9; R. N. Carew Hunt, *The Theory and Practice of Communism* (Baltimore: Penguin Books, 1963), pp. 174–7, 181, 235–6.
65. Leszek Kolakowski, 'The Eurocommunist Schism', *Encounter*, August, 1977, pp. 16–17.

3 THE COMMUNIST PARTIES AND THE INTERNATIONAL BALANCE

1. Indeed, the PCI's own publishing house, Editori Riuniti, published Roy Medvedev's book, *Was the October Revolution Inevitable?*
2. Eric Hobsbawm, *The Italian Road to Socialism: An Interview with Giorgio Napolitano of the Italian Communist Party* (New York: Lawrence Hill and Co., 1977), p. 87 (parentheses added).
3. *The Economist*, November 5–11, 1977, p. 64.

4. Interview in *Corriere della Sera*, Milan, December 30, 1977.
5. *Il Manifesto*, November 1, 1975, p. 2.
6. Don Sassoon, ed., *The Italian Communists Speak For Themselves* (Nottingham: Spokesman, 1978), p. 79.
7. Hobsbawm, *op. cit.*, pp. 57–8 (emphasis and parenthesis added).
8. *Triunfo*, Madrid, July 3, 1976, p. 7.
9. *The Economist*, November 12–18, 1977, p. 14.
10. Leonard Schapiro notes in a paper prepared for this study that Carrillo made a pointed visit to Bucharest at the end of July, 1977, for discussions with Ceausescu at the very time Brezhnev had summoned the bloc general secretaries to join him in the Crimea.
11. Todor Zhivkov, 'Year of Peace, Year of Struggle', *World Marxist Review*, Prague/Toronto, December, 1976, p. 11.
12. Hobsbawm, *op. cit.*, pp. 82–83.
13. *Corriere della Sera*, Milan, May 30, 1976. Also see George Urban, 'Communism With An Italian Face? A Conversation With Lucio Lombardo Radice', *Encounter*, May, 1977, pp. 10, 13, 16.
14. Santiago Carrillo, *'Eurocommunism' and the State* (London: Lawrence and Wishart, 1977), p. 60.
15. *L'Unità*, Rome, March 14, 1972, cited in Foreign Affairs and National Defense Division, Congressional Research Service, Library of Congress, *A Report on West European Communist Parties*, submitted by Senator Edward W. Brooke to the Committee on Appropriations, United States Senate, June, 1977 (Washington, DC: US Government Printing Office, 1977) (hereafter cited as 'Brooke study'), p. 62.
16. *Cahiers du Communisme*, April, 1976, p. 88.
17. The Communist Party of Great Britain, *The British Road to Socialism—Programme of the Communist Party*, London, 1978, p. 43.
18. *L'Unità*, Rome, March 19, 1975, cited in Brooke study, *op. cit.*, p. 62.
19. This caused something of a sensation. Berlinguer's remarks were not reported in the Communist press and the PCI leader went to some trouble to avoid giving the impression that the PCI needed NATO for its own protection. See Michael A. Ledeen, *Italy in Crisis*, The Washington Papers, Vol. 5, No. 43 (Beverly Hills, Cal.: Sage Publications, 1977), p. 46.
20. As long as an accord is not reached to dismantle American and Soviet bases in the whole of Europe. Carrillo interview with the *New York Times*, January 16, 1977, p. 3.
21. Enrico Berlinguer, 'Por un Governo di Svolta Democratica', Rome, 1972, p. 30, cited in Neil McInnes, *The Communist Parties of Western Europe* (London: Oxford University Press, 1975), p. 187.
22. Arrigo Levi, 'Berlinguer's Communism', *Survey*, London, Summer, 1972, p. 9.
23. See, for example, Giuseppe Are, 'Italy's Communists: Foreign and Defense Policies', *Survival*, September–October, 1976.
24. Henry Kissinger, 'Communist Parties in Western Europe', Speech before the Conference on Italy and 'Eurocommunism', American Enterprise Institute, Reprint No. 70 (Washington, DC, 1977), p. 15.
25. *Ibid.*, p. 11.

26. Henry Kissinger, on National Broadcasting Company's 'Today Show',
    January 13, 1978.
27. One of the best illustrations of European-Soviet Communist co-operation
    can be found in the international labour movement. The French Com-
    munist-controlled CGT, for example, runs a training programme jointly
    with the Soviet-controlled WFTU. See Roy Godson, *The Kremlin and
    Labor* (New York: Crane, Russak and Co., Inc., 1977), especially p. 31.
28. *New Times'* attacks upon Carrillo appear only to have reinforced his
    leadership and led to an enlarged Plenum of the Central Committee
    of the PCE which unanimously rejected Soviet criticism. See 'Contrary
    to the Interests of Peace and Socialism in Europe—Concerning the Book
    'Eurocommunism' and the State by Santiago Carrillo, General Secretary
    of the Communist Party of Spain', *New Times*, Moscow, No. 26, June,
    1977. See also 'Putting the Record Straight (re Certain Comments Abroad
    on *New Times* Article About Santiago Carrillo's Book)', *New Times*,
    Moscow, No. 28, July, 1977. When French Communists were singled
    out for their criticism of the Soviet Union (e.g. Jean Elleinstein), the
    French party reminded the Kremlin that the Berlin Conference in 1975
    had decided that criticism of Soviet policies was not to be regarded
    as anti-Communism.
29. *Pravda*, March 18, 1976.
30. Cited by Schapiro.
31. One cannot disregard completely the possibility that some of the differ-
    ences between Moscow and the European parties may have been orches-
    trated specifically to add to the credibility of the European parties.
32. Giuseppe Are, in his paper for this study, emphasizes these points.
33. The best study of a Communist party's finances has been written by
    Jean Montaldo, in *Les Finances Du P.C.F.* (Paris: Albin Michel, 1977).
34. See Roy Godson, *American Labor and European Politics* (New York: Crane,
    Russak & Co., Inc., 1976), p. 82.
35. For a detailed, but unsubstantiated, account, see Victor Riesel's column
    'Red Marines; How Soviet Operatives Got Secret Files to Blackmail
    America's Friends', Field Newspaper Syndicate, August 17, 1976.
36. Schapiro points out that Moscow has charged, incorrectly, that Carrillo
    advocates setting up a Western Europe opposed to the Soviet Union.
    What Carrillo, supported by the PCI and Yugoslavia, has suggested
    is the setting up of a 'neutral' socialist Europe, not tied to either bloc.

Appendix: Research Contributors

THE SOVIET UNION AND THE EUROPEAN COMMUNIST PARTIES

Leonard Schapiro, Professor of Political Science, London School of Economics. Author of numerous books and articles on the Soviet Union, including *The Communist Party of the Soviet Union* (1970) and *Government and Politics of the Soviet Union* (1973)

THE FRENCH COMMUNIST PARTY

Annie Kriegel, Professor of Political Sociology, University of Paris, Nanterre. Author of numerous books on French and European Communism, including *The French Communists* (Chicago, 1972) and *Un Autre Communisme?* (Paris, 1977)

THE ITALIAN COMMUNIST PARTY

Giuseppe Are, Professor of Contemporary History, in the Faculty of Political Science, University of Pisa. Author of numerous studies and articles on the Italian Communists.

THE SPANISH COMMUNIST PARTY

François Bourricaud, Professor of Political Sociology, University Rene Descartes (Sorbonne). Author of numerous books and articles on political and social theory, Southern European and Latin American politics.

Eusebio Mujal-Leon, Center for International Studies, Massachusetts Institute of Technology. Author of numerous articles and monographs on Iberian Communism.

THE PORTUGUESE COMMUNIST PARTY

Rui Machete, Professor of Political Science, Catholic University, Lisbon. Member of Parliament, Social Democratic Party; Minister of Social Affairs, Sixth Provisional Government of Portugal, 1976.

THE BRITISH COMMUNIST PARTY

Dr. Stephen Haseler, Co-author.

Index